Divine W

For business owners and for all
align their purpose

By

Rob Walsh

June 2024

Table of Contents

Introduction

Why this book has been written

This book has come from the inspiration of working with business owners who want to change. It has been driven by close family members who passed away before their time and pushed me to get the message out there.

Who should read it

Everyone needs a reason to read a book, and this one is no exception. It's an essential read for you, whether you are a business owner or not, if you want to fulfil your true purpose in life.

Why you should read this book

The book aims to help you achieve a better alternative to where you are now. It provides clarity on the ways to reach your purpose.

Purpose of the book

If you want change in your life, this book will tell you how to achieve it positively. It will enable you to find and enjoy your purpose and to be in your ultimate flow.

Godly gifts

I don't consider myself Godly and hadn't previously believed I had Godly gifts. But I do now, and that's because of the changes that have occurred in my life.

Godly gifts are:

- given to us by God (our maker) to enable us to make a difference in the world by helping others in goodness and health

- unique talents to help spread the light.

About me

I am a qualified accountant and, in accountancy, you learn numbers; lots of them. Qualification requires taking exam after exam covering various subjects, most of which I've never used in my career or life.

I am also a Christian, and I believe in meditation to help you clear and connect your mind to what you believe in, whether it is God, spirit, energy, the universe or whatever.

How you will achieve your purpose

Divine wisdom led to the purpose I am on and the journey I went on. You can do the same, which is explained in Chapter 1, "Divine — Step 1 to Achieving your Purpose".

My journey was not what I expected

My early qualifications were not as good as expected, so my anticipated career path became impossible. So what could I do then? The initial answer was to panic with sleepless nights and endlessly looking at banking, insurance, or any career options. But what was best?

My godmother, bless her soul, was the National Secretary of the Society of Commercial Accountants and suggested accountancy as a career. I initially thought accountancy was only about numbers and was strictly for nerds.

I had visions of pinstripe suits and social pariahs with no friends. I was wrong. Some of the best human beings are accountants and numbers tell a story, while accounts can illustrate that story.

I studied in Wolverhampton, a place I'd never heard of previously. I stayed in Dudley and suffered terrible home-sickness.

The course covered costing, law, financial reporting and accountancy — foreign languages as far as I was concerned.

But I persevered and eventually gained a credit in a foundation course for accountancy. This allowed me to join a student intake at a small accountancy firm in Bristol.

This was a huge learning curve for me. Credits, debits and extending balances to determine how a business is doing and what tax is due to be paid.

My mentor and guide was called John, a great man and a fellow Bristol City fan. It wasn't all work because, on Friday, we'd spend the swear box money which employees contributed when they came into our room to moan and swear about other employees and clients. We made a small fortune.

What you will learn from this book

This book will tell you how to:

- define your purpose in eight words and why you should do this (Chapter 4):

    ◊ step-by-step guide (Chapter 5)

    ◊ case studies (Chapter 18)

- apply your purpose to your business (Chapter 15)

- embed your purpose with suppliers, your team and customers (Chapters 8-13)

- uphold your values and revisit your purpose (Chapters 14-17)

- measure success (Chapter 18).

If you read this book and apply its lessons, your life and career will change for the better. I hope you enjoy the change!

Author Profile

Rob began his career as a chartered accountant. He worked his way up the ladder over a period of eight years to become a partner in a six-partner firm.

Rob recognised that, as an accountant, he was in an ideal position to not only help business owners to measure their numbers, but also to help them change them and achieve their personal goals. However, he felt he could not do this effectively in his current role. So, in 2003, he formed the Clear Vision Accountancy Group (CVAG) to pursue this vision.

Through CVAG, Rob found his vocation: helping to make a difference in the lives of business owners. He works with them closely, helping them define their goals every year and also assisting in reaching those goals.

He has helped hundreds of business owners to get more of what they want from their lives.

Rob is most definitely a man who 'walks his talk'. He sold the accountancy business five years ago and now helps business owners find their purpose and integrate this into their lives and businesses.

But this success has not been obtained at the expense of Rob's own life — he enjoys thirteen weeks of holiday a year.

Rob hopes you enjoy and benefit from this book. It will help you discover where your business and your life are strong and identify the areas where you can improve. Plus, you will ABSOLUTELY DEFINITELY know where to start to improve your alignment to purpose and attain the life you deserve.

Acknowledgements

I wish to acknowledge the people who have contributed and supported me in creating this book.

First of all, I want to say thank you to my family, who have helped me to be inspired. Thank you to Sue, my wife, and my lovely children, Amy and Chloe, who continue to support me in achieving my goals.

To my parents, Roy and Felicity; you have all been there for me at all times, whether they have been highs or lows.

Thank you to Neil, my brother, and Ben, my nephew, who passed away in the last eight years and have led me to this path.

And thank you to the person who challenged me seventeen years ago about my own eight words.

Thank you to Yvonne Williams, who has been my absolute mentor. And to clients and friends for their humour and knowledge that I'm on a path of difference.

Thank you for the divine intervention and for giving me this direction. And thank you for the Lord's Prayer.

To Jeff Senior, who has been instrumental in helping with the creation of this book.

Dedication

This book is dedicated to all the lovely clients who have shared with me their Purpose and trusted me to be on their journey to fulfil this and their vision.

You have directly contributed to the success of my Purpose and my growth as a human being here to serve.

Dedicated to my lovely Brother Neil and his son Ben, who are undoubtedly helping me on this journey.

Thanks to every one of you.

Preface

When I spent some time at eight and a half thousand feet up in the Himalayas, there were twenty-five peaks around me, and I felt between heaven and earth. This is where I wrote the following poem.

Himalayas

As I gazed over the peaks
The high silent wind streaks
Noisy, quiet but so so pure
Full of wisdom and such a cure
Forests everywhere to be seen
Reaching high to the sky and all so lean
The birds down below whistling their tune
Nowhere to be seen but filling their 'room'
Pure colour in everything up here that's grown
No doubt God's work on what he has sown
I can see for miles and miles
This place continues to make me smile
Will I see a leopard in this beautiful light?
It's beauty in awe - I would not put up a fight!
I am between heaven and earth
- so tranquil, so majestic- this spiritual path
A bird of prey comes to say hello
I think it's a Hobby, so striking and mellow
A yogi lives here with oh so little
orange clothed, thin, humble but full of mettle
Temples here to honour Babaji and others
People come and pay homage in one way or another
I can't contain the love for this striking place
Full of energy and vibration in this holy space
I can see settlements far and wide
Proud inhabitants of this mountainous side

I am feeling the light and connecting me so high
If I had wings I would run and fly
Let me sit a while and see what comes by
But the time has come now to transport myself over the peaks
Seeing so much now I can no longer speak
Thank you oh Lord for this Divine place
It has wisdom and no doubt all your grace.

1

Divine — Step 1 to Achieving your Purpose

"Gratitude is one of the sweet shortcuts to finding peace of mind and happiness inside" (Barry Kaufman)

What is it that determines the course of our lives?

Is it divine intervention that sets us on a certain path?

It certainly is in my case because it dictates the course of my career and my whole life.

What is divine?

Divine is associated with religion and refers to a God or deity. In Latin, it's Divus or Divinus; in old French, it's Dedeus, meaning relating to or coming directly from God. It's something that affects us all, whether we realise it or not.

New ways of working — the background

I started my working career as a trainee accountant but I wasn't a conventional one. After thirteen months, I joined a firm in Bath. They were very rugby-orientated, and I settled in well.

I flourished under the stewardship and mentorship of Tony Swift, a great guy who is still a friend.

He was ahead of his time, and I was lucky to be part of his crusade to change how the big, wide world portrayed accountants, accounting services and accountancy firms. He focused on client service and supporting businesses, which was unheard of in the nineties.

This was the start of feeling different. We were admittedly still doing accounts but setting up different services to help clients.

One was called Anshin, which translates from Japanese as peace of mind, security or reassurance. This was a consultancy company, and only Tony Swift would have thought of it.

This was very interesting because we were going beyond people's businesses to understand their personal goals, business goals, vision, mission, strategies and objectives.

We had some very deep and meaningful conversations. But, most importantly, we were **going behind the numbers to see the true story and looking at their purpose**.

Looking behind the numbers

So what does this mean? Accountants, obviously, do the numbers and clients trust that they're doing them well, that they're helping to save tax where appropriate.

But how do those numbers happen? What is the input into sales, marketing, operations, financial, IT, HR and administration, and what are the outputs? The numbers came from Mesopotamia about 5,000 years ago and were intended to keep track of resources and people. So numbers tell a history of what's happened and, in our case, what makes a business work.

But we need to look at the numbers behind each of those categories:

- sales
- marketing
- operations
- financial
- IT
- HR
- administration.

We need to determine how they make it all work. The relevance of this, of course, is to determine if the business is running you or you are running the business and if the purpose is alive.

Is the business there for all your employees and clients? Yes, of course it is, but it's also there for you. What are your personal goals? What money do you want to earn? It's all about numbers again.

What do you want to achieve in your life, both in business and personally? Although this might seem a bit morbid, what do you want to be said about you on your tombstone?

Would you be glad to work fifty hours a week (to help your clients) if you fulfilled your vision and purpose? (This is described further in Chapter 3, "Purpose").

Following your life's journey

So, after considering this, why is divine relevant? It's because the numbers are leading to questions about your journey, the journey that God put you on this earth for. Let's do an upside-down forecast, starting with personal money to achieve your goals and divine journey.

From personal money, we go to tax, overheads and other costs, then turnover or sales at the bottom. We can then ask ourselves what we need to do to increase personal money by a certain amount to achieve our divine journey in life/our purpose.

This is powerful and feels so right because it enables a discussion about improving ourselves. We can ask how, when, what and who, then get on with our journey.

Defining your vision

God asked us to have a vision for our lives and to see what our life looks like in a specific way. We can do this by asking when, where, who is involved and what is the **purpose**. How will we conduct ourselves? What values will we uphold?

To determine any of this, we can write a vision, such as:

- by 2026, the business will have one million pounds in sales
- it will have ten employees in Bath
- it will make a difference to clients with a motivating, happy team that will uphold our values.

There are so many measurables here. We need to measure:

- the dates
- the **sales**
- the **employees**
- where they're making a **difference**
- the **motivation**
- the **happy team**.

By measuring all of it, we can see where we are on the journey.

But is the vision aligned with our purpose?

Is it A to B in a straight line?

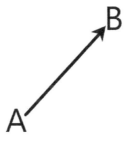

Or is it a wavy line from A to B with a few kinks?

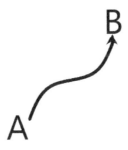

In effect, it's never a straight line because there are always ups and downs, so we just have to keep measuring. If we do, we're helping people to have a vision to pursue and to check in regularly during the journey to see if it all makes sense.

Are we doing God's work for ourselves? This is covered later in Chapter 6, "Why Are We Here On This Earth?".

We achieve the vision by upholding our values.

Adhering to the Commandments' values

We are all aware of the Commandments, but are these the same as our values?

1. I have no other Gods before me.

2. Do not make any graven images.

3. Do not take the name of the Lord in vain.

4. Remember the Sabbath day and keep it holy.

5. Honour your father and mother.

6. Don't kill.

7. Don't commit adultery.

8. Don't steal.

9. Do not bear false witness.

10. Don't covet.

But how relevant are they today? Well, most of them are very relevant for business and life in general.

3. Do not take the name of the Lord in vain

We don't want to be called bad names. We want to uphold our reputation and be respectful in business to employees and clients. Don't allow terms such as "oh my God" to be part of the company's or your personal vocabulary.

4. Remember the Sabbath day and keep it holy

We need rest, and we don't want to be burned out. This is our divine journey; if we do not rest, our physical, emotional and spiritual body will suffer, and we cannot do God's work.

Eat well, exercise well and meditate. Be grateful at all times. Don't be part of the drama, but rise above it. Be at peace and acceptance. Believe your guides and spirits look after you and connect to the higher energy vibration and universe. Sunday is our Day of Rest, so is intended for contemplation, relaxation, and recharging our batteries.

Continue along the next week's journey. Jesus took himself off on the Sabbath, away from all people, to recharge and connect, to be ready to fulfil God's divine work for him.

5. Honour your father and mother

Honour, love and respect your team, clients and suppliers. Don't

---

have an affair with them (because we all know what that means). Have a marriage with them to love and respect them and make the workplace a happy place to be.

6. **Don't kill**
Protect human life in all ways, from health and safety to the Christmas party!!

7. **Don't commit adultery**
Be faithful and be respectful to each other.

8. **Don't steal**
Don't copy your competition, and don't be underhand. Instead, be honourable in all your dealings.

9. **Do not bear false witness**

◊ Don't tell a lie.

◊ Make sure your marketing words do exactly what they say on the tin.

◊ Don't boast, don't over-promise and don't oversell.

◊ Do what you say you will do and, where possible, exceed expectations.

◊ Talk to suppliers, team members and clients respectfully and honestly.

◊ Don't talk behind their back, but say what you mean directly to them, whether face to face, on the telephone or via zoom calls.

◊ Be respectful, and don't tell untrue stories about people. When you lie, you hurt yourself and others, and soon people will not trust what you say.

10. **Don't covet**

Don't use other people's marketing quotes or take the credit for what you did not do. We often want so much to be greedy, but that will badly affect the ethos of the workplace.

So, values in business are like Commandments in the Bible. Be true to them, and they will be true to you.

The relevance of the Commandments

We need to have values in our own lives and business, like the Commandments in the Bible. In our Anshin session, we discussed values to help our clients undertake their journey to uphold and be divine in their duties and deliver their purpose in life.

We helped businesses in all sorts of ways:

- Financial consultancy — knowing their numbers inside out

- Business consultancy — knowing how to run a business

- Strategic consultancy — knowing how to create strategies for the business

- Vision consultancy — helping them to have a vision for their business and personal aims

- Purpose consultancy — helping them find their true purpose

- Alchemistic consultancy —helping them to change to put all of the above in place

- Spiritual consultancy — helping them connect to their spirits and guides.

It's all of them. We are helping each client by investigating their business to pursue a divine journey for them.

So, can an accountancy firm deliver work like this? From the numbers, we can talk about the clients' true divine journeys, by asking questions, listening, listening and listening, and analysing the numbers.

Theory into practice

For example, I was asked to go to a satellite office to help sort it out and put systems and structures in place. It was in a real mess, but it was turned around. They were too busy to do the consultancy work, but it was not forgotten.

The satellite office grew, and I was able to start, many years ago, what were called "Making It Happen" programmes. We started asking questions that we had started through Anshin: vision questions, purpose questions and value questions.

This was the catalyst, but can all clients have the same questions? Of course, they can. Think differently and challenge yourself.

I set up the consultancy arm in the satellite office. Soon, clients were interested and other partners in other offices started to become interested. This was like a movement in accountancy.

An external consultant suggested I do Anshin consulting work over all three offices. Although this was agreed upon, it was not followed through or allowed by the partners because they wanted to do it themselves. A partner started to covet my client's team, and my values were being tested.

Solutions through divine wisdom

There was only one solution to this problem. After asking for divine wisdom, it was delivered. I needed to undertake a buyout of the business in order to follow my purpose, but could I afford it? A way was found. The finance was put in place, the legals were drawn up, and all of the hiccups were being dealt with. The team and the clients stayed loyal to me.

I was starting to practice what I had been preaching. What's my journey, and what does it look like? We called ourselves Clear Vision Accountancy Limited because it represented what we want to do each day:

- provide clarity

- provide vision

- help their journey, both for team members and clients

- the vehicle to stand, to start to perform.

Divine work was nearly in place.

The vision was put in place by 2020 to have 75 ideal clients provide one million pounds of turnover with a happy, service-orientated team, delivering unique services to clients and making a difference.

This flowed from within me. This was the moment.

- What gifts have I been given to help people to get them to a better place?

- How can I serve?

- How can I deliver?

This was a light bulb moment. Divine inspiration as described previously on page one. My purpose was 'breathing'.

Would I deem myself as Godly? No. Would I deem myself as having Godly gifts in the past and now? Yes.

Using God-given gifts

So, where did this come from? From my head, my soul or divine wisdom? What was the connection to hearing, sensing, feeling, holding the energy, and then speaking?

Not just hearing but really listening without thinking of my next question. To let go of ego, to sense, to ask the right questions, but not yet. To feel, to really feel, to connect with them, to let their emotions speak to me, to be empathetic. To sit in their seat, to feel their energy and their vibration. To hold their space and let them flow.

To let myself flow free of ego, free of making a drama point. Just say what flows naturally. When I'm in flow, I feel that I have left my body. I'm in spirit with energy and being a person that I didn't even recognise at that time, but now I do.

I'm free of conflict. Delivering in a kind and empathetic way to allow people to trust me and feel safe. There's a formula, which is:

- trust = intimacy (caring) + reliability (consistency) + credibility.

Believe in what you do and deliver. Was this truly me? A drinking, ex-rugby player connecting in such a way that I'd never experienced before.

Where did this come from? A gift, a special gift from God. I'm grateful every day, and I practice this virtually every day.

This consultancy business grew, and a great connection took place, and wisdom followed. At the next stage, we were integrating this into the accounting business and we coached the team.

Some team members loved it; some didn't; that was to be expected. Clients loved the work, and the Operations Manager became the Operations Director, which released even more time to focus on the consultancy.

A journey through divine intervention

My Non-executive Director asked me to describe in eight words why I am here. My answer was immediate — "Because I care to make a bloody difference" (see Chapter Four, "Eight Words").

My brother passed away suddenly, and anxiety kicked in. Since then, I've been on a journey:

- hypnotherapy
- retreat
- yoga
- who am I?

- what am I?

- meditation

- spiritual mediumship

- emotional mastery.

There were hardly any books but lots of feelings. Asking my heart and soul for the right step, the next step, what's my journey and what's delivered?

Then, wham bam, I had heart issues. This was probably caused by stress, maybe being overweight and drinking. It was definitely due to caring for others rather than looking after myself enough. My heart rate went up to 170 against a normal rate of 60-100 at rest, and it wouldn't go down.

I experienced four episodes and two ambulances in a foreign country. But, a few minor operations later, all appeared good.

It happened again on Boxing Day, December 2018. I remember looking up in the A&E ward to the white light in the ceiling before I was knocked out to have my heart put back into rhythm. How did I get here?

Everything moved on quickly from there. But, eight days later, the Operations Director handed in his notice in order to run an accountancy business. I asked him immediately to buy me out. There was no hesitation, so this was definitely Divine Intervention.

Pastures new

The deal was done six months later, but had I sold my baby too soon?

I was having separation issues. Synchronicities happen. Spirits connected to me from a medium and said this was my journey, and I must not look back. I was off to pastures new.

So that's where we are now, delivering every day after hearing, sensing, feeling, holding the energy and speaking in a tone that I have been given.

Kind, jovial, caring and inspirational, hopefully. I'm a grateful and contented human being and have energy, which is no doubt a divine gift with divine inspiration, leading to divine wisdom.

What changes have I experienced, and what lessons have I learned in this chapter?

1. The journey.

2. Don't be afraid.

3. Don't let your ego get in the way.

4. Be present.

5. Go with the flow.

6. Know that divinity is within all of us — our soul, our holy spirit.

This leads me to Chapter Two, "Wisdom".

2
Wisdom

"Worrying does not empty tomorrow of its sorrow. It empties today of its strength" (Corrie Ten Boom)

What is wisdom?

The definition of wisdom is:

- the quality of having experience, knowledge and good judgment
- the quality of being wise
- the fact of being based on sensible or wise thinking
- the body of knowledge and experience that develops within a specified society.

So, where does wisdom come from?

It comes from a combination of things:

- DNA
- age
- experience.

Is it from layers that are gradually unearthed? Or do we gain wisdom from failure? Or could it be a combination of the above?

Wisdom: — wise — knowledge— experience— failure/age.

Why do we talk of being as wise as an owl? Why is wisdom linked to an owl?

Is it because it has 360-degree sight? What about referring to a wise old owl? Is it because wisdom comes from age?

All-knowing, but why all-knowing?

Where does knowing come from?

Knowing most things comes from experiences.

But what is an experience?

It's one that you remember in your lifetime, one you can recollect when you can remember the details, the situation, the why, the who, the how and the picture of it.

We have mental maps that we create for our experiences. So, what's a mental map?

A mental map

All our experiences and interpretations are built into mental maps, and we believe they are truth or reality. But they're really only the best guess we can achieve at that point in time and are based on previous best guesses, which in turn are based on earlier best guesses. They're based on experiences we have no recollection of, which are based on other tools that our brain created while in the womb.

We call these reconstructions mental maps. We use mental maps for everything because they help us go through life without having to discover a journey all over again. We don't have to re-analyse everything each time we come across it.

Everything we know, we know because we have a mental map about it. If I say the word 'table', we'll have a mental map about it, but each of us has a slightly different one, which depends on our experience, education, et cetera. But we also have mental maps for how we choose our next job, how we treat our clients, how we pick our life partner, how we're being a parent, how we choose food from a menu and so on.

Each mental map is neither right nor wrong. It is what it is. We adopted it at a certain point in our lives because, at that point, it helped us make sense of reality in a successful way. We adopted it, and we stuck with it. We're using it as many times as possible.

Most mental maps have been helping us amazingly well. But what happens now? As we grow and develop, we change some mental maps that used to serve us well because they become less helpful or even harmful.

But since we've been using them for so many years, it's hard for us to see it. We blame reality for making us unhappy, but our mental maps play a huge part in determining our whole experience of life.

So, if mental maps create experiences, does this lead to wisdom? No, it's part of it. It's like a formula.

Knowing = experiences + failures + learnings + age + intuition = wisdom.

Is this the equation? Maybe.

Failures

This is in your own mind. One must have attempted something which was not successful, but was it? How many failures must we have before success is achieved?

A driving test or an exam; maybe we were not ready to pass, to make a success of it.

I had four attempts to pass my driving test, and I learned from my failures.

Failure leads to knowledge but not wisdom. Is wisdom a higher form of knowledge? Failure is definitely part of the equation.

Do learnings come from failures?

Yes, they do.

Learning is something you remember that will help you in the future. You pass on the knowledge to yourself for the future and can share it with others for the future. I've had many learnings:

1. I'm not good at DIY.

2. If, in business, I make a decision that is not aligned with my purpose and vision, then it is wrong.

3. Employing the wrong people.

4. Avoiding confrontation since it still has to be dealt with later.

So learnings = experiences = create mental maps.

Our learnings are definitely part of wisdom.

Age

Can we say that the older you are, the more wisdom you have? We can, in some cases.

But many people have wisdom far beyond their years. So the question is, why is that?

Is wisdom built into the DNA of people? I think it is, but it probably comes out with age.

You can see intuition.

I think age is definitely part of wisdom because it gives us experiences/learnings, and failures. We talk about my wise old gran, about a wise old sage.

So, at what age do we become wise? We're learning every second, minute, hour, day, month and year.

Time = age = wisdom.

DNA

So, are we built with wisdom in our DNA (Godly gifts)? Yes.

Did it come out at different times and at different ages? In my view, yes, it did

How do we find out? Do we need to find out or just accept it?

What do we need to do to trigger the release of our wisdom (DNA)? Experience a situation, a trauma? Maybe yes.

There are people with children who have life-threatening illnesses, and they become wise beyond their years because of their situation.

So does the wisdom come out earlier than it otherwise would have done because they know that they're passing from this lifetime?

These inspiring people pass their wisdom on in so many ways, and their stories are there in the newspapers, so it must be in their DNA, that so-called wisdom in DNA.

Intuition and wisdom

How are intuition and wisdom linked?

Gut feel/heart feeling = intuition.

Let's look at the concept of the second brain, scientifically known as the gut. Early organisms did not have complex brains, and so developed using their gut, which is where the idea of gut feeling comes from. Studies have shown the synapses in the brain are very similar to those in the gut and effectively work in the same way.

In knowing right from wrong, what is right/wrong? Who knows? How do we know what's good and what's bad?

As mentioned in the previous chapter, I had a series of heart issues where atrial fibrillation sent my heart rate up to 170, and it wouldn't come down. After two trips in ambulances to hospitals abroad, an operation was performed and it appeared to solve the problem. So that appeared to be a good outcome.

Then the problem re-occurred, so that was bad.

Medication was prescribed, and this seemed to work, so again, it was good.

One day, the condition happened yet again, and the medication wasn't working. I was in an A&E department, looking up at the white fluorescent lights and thinking how did I get here? So this was bad, one would think.

But a successful procedure was quickly performed, and the situation was good again. Then, four days later, somebody handed their notice in at my place of work, which again was bad, one would think.

But it made me think about the business, about whether to sell it and move on as part of my journey. We agreed on a price, and I sold the business, and then I went on to pastures new, creating a difference for many people. So this was good.

How do you know whether anything is bad or good? It may seem bad at the time, but it may turn into something that's good.

How can we label good or bad, right or wrong? That's what the key to this point is.

So, is this the same thing? Is intuition the same thing as wisdom?

Remember the definition of wisdom. It is:

- the quality of having experience, knowledge and good judgment
- the quality of being wise
- the fact of being based on sensible or wise thinking
- the body of knowledge and experience that develops within a specified society.

The definition of intuition is the ability to understand something instinctively without the need for conscious reasoning. We shall allow our intuition to guide us. A thing that one knows or considers likely from instinctive feeling rather than conscious reasoning.

Is this wisdom? So, is this the same thing?

See how to interlink intuition and wisdom. Wisdom is gained from experiences, while intuition is already within us. Tap into source and soul.

Our intuition is really within us, and already, we have some wisdom, and this is within our DNA. So definitely, yes.

So, what have we learned in this chapter? Wisdom is from the Divine, whether it is from:

- failure
- mistakes
- learnings
- DNA
- experiences
- intuition
- age.

It's all the same, I believe, just with different labels.

The outcome, therefore, is that wisdom comes from all of it.

3
Purpose

"Your passion is your purpose. And your purpose is to serve"
(Anon)

Purpose, family, friends, business, life, charity, wealth.

What is the definition of purpose?

It's the reason for which something is done or created, for which something exists. It's a person's sense of resolve or determination, how one meets one's intentional objective.

To be of use in life, have a purpose for your family:

- security
- support
- love
- growth
- care
- fun.

Have the same purpose for your friends.

Have a purpose in business. What is this?

- make money
- provide jobs for families
- train people
- maximise their skills
- provide legacy money for their families.

Leave a legacy yourself. You may want to make a mark on this planet: to be rich, to have wives or husbands, to have love, to have boats, watches, homes or other material possessions.

Purpose and identity

But where do we lose our identity? Is it really our business purpose to embrace the carbon footprint, to simply provide a service or goods to humanity? Do we really want to encourage a habit such as sugar consumption, gambling, vaping, chocolate, sex or alcohol?

Everyone has a need, but whether it's authentic or not, there is a demand, and we want to provide a service. This may be an authentic purpose but is it a true business purpose to feed on the weak or the vulnerable? Is this what boardrooms are there for: to make money out of the vulnerable, the weak, and the mentally ill?

When does a purpose get lost?

Where does ego conflict with purpose? Does it?

Is it in trying to maximise shareholder returns? Is it trying to increase market share?

Great, if it's an authentic service for good. But not so great if it's about power, money, ego and feeling vulnerable.

What is a business purpose? To do right by its employees, shareholders, suppliers, customers and the environment in an authentic and value-driven way. That's it. And it should be this at all times.

When you start a business, do you look at the opportunity, or do you look at your purpose in life?

What is it? What do you actually do? When an opportunity comes along, do you see if it fits your purpose, or do you just go for it?

Remaining true to God's purpose

To illustrate what your purpose in life should be, here's an article that featured on the *A Word In Due Season* website:

ANYWHERE, ANYTIME, ANY COST

Scripture: Matthew 26:8 "When the Disciples saw it, they had indignation, saying, To what purpose is this waste?"

While Jesus was sitting down for a meal with his Disciples a woman approached Him carrying an alabaster box that contained very precious ointment. This small box of ointment was worth about a year's wages. When she began to pour this precious ointment upon Jesus' head, it caused much turmoil amongst His Disciples. They could not see the purpose of this act and felt that it was very wasteful, for the ointment could have been sold and the proceeds given to the poor. Jesus commended the woman's actions, however, by saying, "Why do you trouble the woman? For she has done a good work upon Me ... She did this for My burial."

It would take many of us several years to save up a year's salary because after we pay our bills and necessities each month, we have very little left over. For me, it would be a great temptation to dip into those funds every time a special need came up. Yet somehow this woman was able to save the ointment for this occasion even though she may not have understood at the time why she was even saving it. She probably never dreamed that God had a special purpose or that He was going to use her gift to honor His Son. It is said, "What we receive too cheaply, we esteem too lightly." To her, Jesus was worth every drop of this expensive ointment, so she did not count the cost as a loss. While others esteemed her actions as waste, she esteemed her sacrifice as an honor to the Son of God.

There was a man from India who came to America in hopes of a better life. His dream came true and after many years he had gained a prosperous and wonderful life. Yet, God called him to give up everything and return to his poverty-stricken homeland to minister. After a season of struggling with the desires of his own soul, he obeyed God's command. He made a commitment to God declaring, "Anywhere, Anytime, Any Cost."

We must understand that God's purposes are not designed to fit our lives, but our lives are meant to fit His purposes. *We may not understand the things that are happening in our lives, but we can be sure that the things we are going through are producing precious ointment within our souls. Even though we do not have an alabaster box that is filled with precious ointment, but we do have a heart and it should be filled with a desire to do God's will. If we give our all to the Lord, every sacrifice that we make will be used in its season for His glory. Others may question our sacrifice and have indignation because they see our gift or sacrifice as a waste,* **but we must remain true to God's purpose and be ready when He is ready.** *Our commitment should always be "Anywhere, Anytime, Any Cost."*

Charitable purpose

As an example, let's look at charitable purposes. Do we give money because it's easy to do? Or do we give our time to help things nurture and grow?

How much pro bono work do we do to help people nurture and grow, to have a ripple effect on the world? Helping one person who helps a few means they can help many who help even more. So even a small effort can contribute to the overall help.

But time is a Godly gift so you can use your divine wisdom to help a charity achieve its goals and ambitions — perfect. Or do we give money to a charity that is already set up? As long as it's authentic.

Should we all have a charitable purpose? Definitely, yes. Again, the purpose is to be useful, to have meaning.

Purpose in life

Why are you here on this earth? Why do you do what you do? Are you aligned with your purpose?

If we consider a spine:

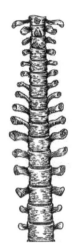

If all the vertebrae are in a straight line and correctly aligned, there's no problem. If, however, any of the vertebrae move out of line, you will experience pain and mobility issues, so there are problems.

So which are you?

If you view your business in terms of a spine, each vertebrae will be an element of the business — purpose, vision, strategy, goals, structure, and sales. Marketing, operational, finance, administration, IT and HR.

Purpose
Vision
Strategy
Goals
Structure
Sales
Marketing
Operational
Finance
Administration
IT
HR

All of these elements need to be aligned with the purpose. If your purpose is not in alignment with your HR strategy, you'll be employing the wrong people.

You'll be attracting the wrong people. You'll have people coming and going. You have to make sure that your purpose is indoctrinated in the DNA of your business.

Again, that term DNA. DNA is within your spine, within the vertebrae, so you have to make sure that everything's aligned with the top vertebrae, which is purpose.

If you have a back problem, if your top vertebrae is out of alignment, that then forces the rest of your spine out of alignment. Even your hips, your legs and your knees are affected. If the top two vertebrae are out of alignment, then suddenly, this makes it even worse.

If you've got a lot of vertebrae out of alignment, you're obviously in a lot of pain; then the business is all over the place.

You can see when you walk into any business where the purpose is shining through, and everyone and everything is connected.

I've helped many people with their purpose, and sometimes it needs a tweak. Sometimes, it needs a complete restructure. Sometimes, they don't know what their purpose is, or if they do, it's just lost somewhere.

Employees' purpose

Then we come back to employees. They have a purpose, but do they know what their purpose is?

This is illustrated by a Buddhist saying:

> *A man walks by a mason working on a cathedral. He asks him what he's doing. The mason says: "I'm making money so I can send it home."*

> *Next day, the man walks by again and there's a different mason. He asks: "What you doing?" The mason replies: "I'm making*

money so that I can then set up my business and provide for my family."

Next day, the man walks along and there's a third mason so he asks: "What you doing?" The mason says: "I'm creating a cathedral where many people will worship for many, many years. I'm part of that and I'm proud to be part of that."

How different is that? That's his purpose. That's his cathedral. That's what he came to work on every day.

Similarly, consider an NHS cleaner in a hospital. Is he cleaning, or is he saving lives?

There are many things and many purposes we share. Even though we have a mundane job, it's our purpose. If people love what they do, you can see it. There's a light in their eyes because they have a true purpose. They are in flow.

Aligning purpose

So, if a vertebrae is out of place, or even if we pop the cartilage in between, there is pain, and we have to deal with it — operation, physio, chiropractor.

Do you know when you are out of alignment with your purpose? Does the job feel the same? Do the people feel the same? Are the business owners still the same people who started the business?

People change, but their values should not. If you know the values have changed in a business, somebody is misaligned. Should you stay or go? You may be offered more money to stay, but company values have changed for the worse.

Do you stay? Where are you aligned? Is this your true purpose? Is it to take money to just stay in the same job. It's a big decision but do you know what's right?

Purpose has a value, and there's an alignment. When you're not synchronised, then you have to alter your path. You have to leave yourself and look at yourself to see if you are aligned. If not, then move on. Talk to someone regarding your purpose.

It's about building, and this purpose is linked to who we are, to our DNA and to our purpose in life.

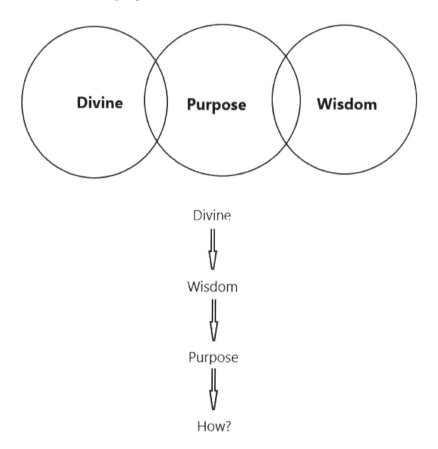

So, the question of how we achieve this is dealt with in the next chapter.

4
Eight Words

I focus on eight words not simply as a random number but because eight has a certain significance.

The Significance of eight

We can see eight words not in the context of a normal eight but in other ways. If we turn the number eight sideways, it can be seen as the infinity symbol:

Or it can be seen as two bodies.

Infinity is defined as something that is unlimited, endless, and without bounds. It is an eternity or a ribbon that has no ends or beginnings. The affinity symbol in Japanese is considered to be lucky. It gives the idea that growth is linked with prosperity.

There is great symbolism attached to the number eight, and it is spiritual. Spiritual represents anything that is infinite, whether it be countless ideas in your head or the depth of your emotion.

The number eight is also believed to be the balance between the materialistic and the spiritual aspects of an individual. The main focus of this number is to gain success, be ambitious, and have every level of life.

The meaning of eight

Eight is a number associated with:

- material freedom

- a financial abundance of wealth

- compassion

- self-reliance

- independence and freedom

- confidence

- inner wisdom

- personal power and/or privacy

- being professional

- insightful and spiritual consciousness.

Your company's purpose in eight words

Seth Godin, in his great marketing book *Purple Cow: Transform Your Business by Being Remarkable*, states that companies must build things worthy of notice into their products or services.

So, in eight words, why do you sell what you do? Why are you here on this earth?

This is defining your purpose. So, in eight words, ask yourself:

- **Why am I here on this earth?**

- **Why do I do what I do?**

Over the years, I've asked these questions to many clients. Seventeen years ago, I was asked the same questions, and my eight words were: *Because I care to make a bloody difference.*

Going the extra mile

I read a question by Deepak Chopra: "Would you change your job to align to your purpose?". My immediate answer was 'no' because the job I was in, the life I was leading, was definitely my purpose. So I didn't even have to think about changing my job.

So, my response was immediate because I care to make a bloody difference. But is it subjective, or is it in the DNA of who we are?

So if I break down the words 'Because I care', care means always going the extra mile.

Many businesses say on their website and in their marketing material that they have a care programme. So, I often ask what the care programme means. They say to me that they're doing this, they're doing that. They're supporting their employees.

One company allowed an employee to work from the offices because at home it was too noisy and he could not study. I asked the owner of the business if he organised coffee or takeaway food for this employee so he could be fed whilst he was studying. That's going the extra mile, but he said 'no'.

So, I gave him examples of what care actually means. As a result, he marked his care programme down from ten out of ten to six out of ten, meaning he has to work harder.

Taking care

If you look at the word care, think of it as:

- **C**ourtesy
- **A**ttitude
- **R**elationship
- **E**xcellence.

Consider each part of this:

- Courtesy requires you to be courteous at all times to everybody — clients, suppliers, team members and all others you come in contact with.

- Attitude means bringing your best attitude to work, being better than you were yesterday, and just doing that extra one percent.

- Relationships are built with your fellow team members and your clients. So make sure that, whatever you say about people, you do it to their face and not behind their back. Make the interactions memorable.

- Excellence is achieved by being excellent in all that you do and by striving to do better each day.

Care is part of my eight words, and courtesy, attitude, relationships and excellence are basically what was brought into the business.

Persistence pays

If we further consider my eight words *Because I care to make a bloody difference*, what does *make* actually mean in a business sense?

It means taking action, acting on intuitions, doing things, learning and follow ups. It means making sure you get noticed, planning, detail, following up, being sure you say 'please' and 'thank you' and checking all your communications.

Then there's the word *bloody*. It implies being determined. Not giving up; being consistent and persistent.

I wasn't allowed to put the word 'bloody' in my marketing language. However, later on, I was persistent, and I got it in there; on my website and everywhere else, I use the eight words.

Actually making a difference

Finally, there's the word *difference*.

We made a difference, and we did it in many ways. This included our rooms. We changed the title of the rooms to 'big difference rooms' and 'small difference rooms'.

We ask for feedback on whether we'd made a total difference to clients in the year. A big difference, small difference or no difference at all. We went the extra mile, and we started to get noticed for the work we do.

That included the drinks service. We had a menu of drinks available when people walk into the reception.

We had a red carpet for new clients who came in from the car park. We had a jukebox that they could play records on. And, when they played a record, we made a note of it so that the next time they came into the offices, we put the same record on again.

And they noticed; that's a difference, that's care.

So then we put it into our sales packages. We gave our clients the option of having a:

- total difference service package

- big difference service package

- small difference service package

- no difference service package.

The no-difference service package is just pure compliance, pure accounts and tax. The small difference package is accounts, tax and maybe management accounts whereas the big difference package also has forecasts, management accounts and bookkeeping; the whole shebang.

The total difference package adds consultancy — purpose consultancy, vision consultancy, strategy consultancy — all to make a total difference.

Then we got feedback from these clients to see what difference it made, whether it was no, small, big or a total difference, and we put that on the website.

If clients don't want to be different, then fine. They can leave or be a compliance client only. There is no judgment here.

Worthy of notice

The significance of the eight words' meaning is a concept of limitlessness or eternity linking to infinity. It's about two bodies coming together. It represents anything that is infinite, whether that be the countless ideas in your head or the depth of your emotions.

As Seth Godin says: "We notice what we choose to notice."

So, that comes down to the purpose of the individual. Hence, the reason for the eight words and it's very definite connection to infinity and its meaning: eight — infinity, limitless purpose. That's what I have learned and shared in this chapter.

In the next chapter, you'll learn **how** to determine your eight words.

5
How Do You Do the Eight Words?

There are two main questions relevant to how you define your eight words:

- Why do you do what you do?

- Why are you here on this earth?

So, you need to pick words out and listen to them repeatedly to see if they work.

Determining the eight words

As an example of how you determine your eight words, there's a lady in Ibiza who is a medicine woman who travels the world performing ceremonies. She started off with different words in her purpose.

Her words were:

- create

- opening

- safe

- inspire

- true authentic self.

We wrote down the words, and I asked her to write the first sentence about her purpose in eight words. It wasn't eight words; it was twenty.

So, she wrote a sentence, and I wrote a sentence about her purpose. We compared them, and then we went again and rewrote the sentence. We repeated the process, and then, after writing and comparing sentences three and four, I asked whether the latest version was motivational and represented her true self.

We finally decided on a version that was motivational and achieved a satisfactory outcome. *Her purpose is to create a doorway* and a safe space for our human heart to heal, reconnect and inspire to celebrate our life and expand our true, authentic selves.

We had to then go through each sentence, each part of the purpose to see whether we could measure it.

I am creating a doorway. What does that mean? Basically, she's creating an opportunity for people to talk about going through the doorway to change their lives.

She is doing it in a safe space, and she can measure the safe space. She can measure the feedback from the people there in the ceremonies to see if they've healed, reconnected or are inspired. To see what they're celebrating in their life and whether they're going to grow and expand.

This is how she's phrased her purpose:

With my love, voice, songs and healing energy, I am <u>creating</u> <u>doorways</u>, a passage, a temple of safety <u>where our human</u> <u>hearts</u> individually and as a community <u>can heal</u> and find rest from the chatting and control of our minds. Where we reconnect to the life force within us and where we can find new inspiration for our lives and path.

My work with groups and individuals is creating a high vibrational, ceremonial spaces celebration, an expansion of our true, authentic selves that was beyond our thoughts and patterns. That was pure love. We are pure love. And with this clarity comes the wish to spread out more and more, near and far in different ceremonies and ways. I'm open to create magic and unique collaborations in these times we live in to awaken and inspire as humans.

The key eight words are those underlined in the first sentence.

Always the same process

So this is an example recently of how I conducted the exercise on eight words. I always start off with those two questions:

- Why do you do what you do?

- Why are you here on this earth?

Then, literally, it's a process of pen and paper. Words and words, make a sentence, go again and again until it's what we want. What's his or her purpose?

Ask them whether they feel it's motivational, then see if it can be measured, and then get them to recite it. You can always tell when a person has their purpose aligned because they can recite their eight words, and they live by those eight words.

This lady has 24 words. Every time I go on a Zoom call with her, she basically knows them probably at eight, nine and sometimes at ten out of ten. She's living her purpose, although in her case, it's 24 words. She's now put this into her marketing and into her Facebook account.

This is the process. All you have to do is be there to **hold the space**, to **feel the energy**, to **pick out the words** and **help to create something**. Normally, this takes less than two hours, and you can see during those two hours when the light comes on, and then you know they've got their purpose.

It's a truly inspirational and lovely moment. I help people align themselves with their purpose on a regular basis. It is extremely fulfilling, and that's why I am not retiring yet —there's too much to help with!!

6
Why Are We Here On This Earth?

There are different concepts and different opinions as to why we are here on this earth. Are we just a ball of continuous energy that has dropped into the physical being to experience all emotions, hardship, learnings and experiences. All the sights we can see until the next life.

Have we been here before?

Are we here to leave a legacy? Is it to help others? Is it to continue the human race? Is it to deal with our purpose?

There are some people who believe they've been here before. One person I know believes that, in a previous life, he was shot in the neck, and so he hates having things around his neck. But who knows whether that's true or not?

Leaving a legacy

What does leaving a legacy mean?

Is it family? Is it wealth? Is it clarity? What matters?

To have a legacy on your tombstone, what words would you choose? That should define your purpose and why you're here on this earth. Spike Milligan, the famous comedian, had the words *I told you that I was ill* inscribed on his tombstone.

So why are we here on this earth? Is it God's will? The Bible urges you to follow God's plan for your lives.

It can seem insurmountable, and maybe we wish we had a detailed roadmap we could follow, which outlines every decision we make in our lives. But, if we were sent a map if it existed, would it steal away the dependency on God and the need to learn? So are you here on earth to do God's work, to love, to grow into faith, to develop gifts and to serve?

Is it to do good work for others? To remain pure, to love, to remain free. And to remain free from the love of money, also to share good news with others.

What do you believe in Christ's work? I believe I'm here on this earth to serve God's purpose. For me, being shown areas in life to grow, to fail, to learn, to grow again and make a difference. To achieve my eight words: *Because I care to make a bloody difference*, in my case.

Being without ego

You have to be without ego. It's very important.

Once, I set up a podcast called *Advisors Anon,* and the concept was that no names were mentioned. The interviewer — no name, the interviewee — no name, the business — no name.

Basically, the whole podcast was concerned with talking for 22 minutes about what they were passionate about in life. This went on to different podcasts and on to Apple and Spotify.

People listened to it from all around the world. There was no sales, no marketing and, more importantly, no ego.

Are you here on this earth to have a huge effect, or is it a ripple effect? Do you help a massive group at one time to have a big effect? Or do you work with one person who is very well connected in a small group and then put the message out to his or her small group? That's a ripple effect, which I prefer.

Making a difference

So why are you here on this earth? Is it to help many people?

There is a lady in New York; she's a psychotherapist who helps families in New York State. She deals with adolescents who have mental health problems and helps the parents cope with those problems. So her eight words are: *Change the way mental health is taught in USA.*

She started writing a book. She's now written a 21 chapter book that she turned into 21 lessons for schools, which turned into 21 homework lessons for their classes and which then turned into 21 assessments for teachers. Assessors can see, in the language of the students, whether they're writing words that show they're in mental health decline.

She's also written a teacher training guide for these 21 classes, and she's going to try it out in New York State. She's coming to Scotland next year to meet Members of Parliament and Education Ministers. We're hoping to get it set up in England as well.

Now, how can those eight words have such an effect on an individual? That they spawn this huge energy within her?

These eight words have taken over her life because she believes it's her true purpose, and she's going all guns blazing to achieve those goals. Who knows whether she's achieved it, but at least she's making a difference. And this is how one purpose basically can help change the world. It's a new light dawning.

People like this are making a difference. If we look at accountants and any other businesses, they have clients that they do numbers for. If they can focus on helping those clients focus on their purpose, then they are making a difference to them, to their friends, to their family, and the ripple effect starts. It's huge.

Why are we here?

So, these are just a few examples of why people are here on this earth, and there will be many more examples later in the book. So what we learned is:

- Believe in what you believe in

- Focus

- Have an intention and do it

- Don't beat yourself up if you don't get to the right place

- Get to flow.

What is flow? It's your total free state that shows and allows you to be who you truly are (your authentic self) and why you are truly here. It's a state of mind where you become fully immersed in an activity.

So why are we here? Are we here to experience the physical and to make sure we achieve our destiny and purpose, however hard it may be? To be authentic whilst here and not to exploit people. To experience beautiful tastes, wonderful views, extreme feelings, wonderful music and sounds and lovely smells. To view all that God has created, to hone your skills and to become the best you can be.

Be kind, be caring, be loving, be compassionate and be generous. Be yourself, be present and at all times, don't get hooked up in this fast-paced world.

7
Why Do You Do What You Do?

So why do you do what you do?

Is it by chance? Is it necessary? Is it for money? Is it for the family business?

Are you stuck in a rut? Is it for training? Is it your journey? Or is it God's choice for your path, such as Moses and Abraham, who had to wait many years before God gave them the life that he chose for them?

Happiness through alignment with purpose

So why do we do what we do?

How many of us are following our purpose? How many of us are enjoying work? How many of us are truly happy? How many of us are happy at work? How many are happy with money? How many of us are happy with our relationships? How many of us are happy with our marriage?

It's basically those who are aligned with their purpose.

Is this due to divine intervention? Is it knowing what you know at an early stage? If it is, then you do what you do.

Is it being in the right place at the right time? Synchronicity.

Why do you do what you do? Is it for the sense of achievement? Is it for fulfilment? Is it for happiness?

Look at nurses. They are so caring, and they do what they do. Look at the cleaners in the hospitals and why they do what they do.

If you ask them, some may say they're just doing their job. Some may say they're just cleaning. Some may say they're saving lives each day by preventing infections and so forth.

Why do florists do what they do? Is it because they have a sense of colour and they are creative?

Flourishing rather than languishing

Sometimes, we do what we do to become better, to flourish. The *United Christian Broadcasters* website, in its *The UCB Word for Today* feature, had an illustration of this, as follows:

Are you flourishing?

"They will flourish in the courts of our God."

Psalm 92:13 NIV

Inside you there's a battle between your flourishing self – the person you were created to be – and your languishing self.

'What's that?' you ask. Your languishing self feels uneasy and discontent. You're drawn to bad habits like mindlessly watching TV, drinking too much, misusing sex, excessive spending – things designed to temporarily anaesthetise pain. Your thoughts automatically drift in the direction of fear and anger.

Learning doesn't feel worthwhile. You think about yourself most of the time.

Whereas flourishing [thriving, blossoming, and prospering] takes place:

*1) In your spirit. You sense you're beginning to receive ideas and energy from an outside source. And you are. You're being empowered by God's Spirit. We talk about being inspired, which literally means 'God breathed'. God breathes into you; you come alive and feel like you've a **purpose for living**.*

2) In your mind. Your thoughts are marked by joy and peace. You have a desire to love and to learn. You're literally being transformed by 'the renewing of your mind' (Romans 12:2 NIV).

3) In your time. You wake each day with a sense of excitement, and you realise you're never too young to flourish. Mozart was composing brilliant music when he was five. Paul told Timothy, 'Don't let anyone look down on you because you are young' (1 Timothy 4:12 NIV).

You also realise you're never too old to flourish. Grandma Moses was sixty-nine when she took up painting, and artist Marc Chagall did some of his best work in his nineties.

It's humbling to acknowledge you can't be anything you want. But once you accept that and **seek to maximise what God created you to be***, you start flourishing.*

Finding our true purpose

Somebody I'm aware of was an opera singer and going higher and higher in the world of opera, singing at different places in England and then into Europe. She was destined for a huge future as an opera singer. One night, she had a car crash, and for some strange reason, her throat was affected, and her vocal cords were damaged, never to be repaired.

She obviously was devastated, and then she had a calling to Chinese medicine, Chinese health, and Chinese Vedic charting. She went on a journey, learning all about the stars in the sky at different times of the year and on our birthdays, and could then give you a chart of what is in your life.

She became involved in Chinese medicine and started helping people. She's now very famous. She's providing readings for the stars, and she's helping. She has a website selling herbal remedies for many ailments. Obviously, it was very exciting being an opera singer, but she turned it around.

So, was her true purpose to be a singer? Obviously not. Now, she's doing what she's doing in Chinese medicine and healing.

Work-life balance

So why do we do what we do? Is it in our mental maps? (mentioned in Chapter 2, "Wisdom"). Is it in our DNA? Is it due to our history?

If it's our purpose, then it just flows from one thing to another when we're at work. And living a life to its fullest.

Do you work to live, or do you live to work? Somebody asked me this question about work-life balance. I answered: "If you are doing your purpose every day, how can you tell the difference between work and life?".

If you're doing your purpose, it's the same thing. And, in my case, if I do my eight words, it's *because I care to make a bloody difference*. Then I'm doing it all the time, whether it's in work or whether it's in life.

So therefore, working to live or living to work; if you're following your ideal purpose, there is no difference, and you need to realise that. Don't focus on your holidays, don't focus on Fridays and don't focus on Mondays because they're all the same thing.

Ask yourself this question: Are you working to live, or are you living to work? And then, link that to your current career and see if you're following your purpose.

For myself, I was supposed to be going into banking and international finance, getting a degree at Loughborough or London universities. My A levels were not good, even though I worked really hard. I had bad grades — D, E and O — and then I had no idea what my purpose was. And then my godmother recommended doing accountancy at Wolverhampton Polytechnic.

So off I went to do an accountancy foundation and that started my journey for one year. Accountancy has led me to learn so many different things from financials to planning, to strategy, to vision and to purpose. Therefore, **why I do what I do is because of that journey**.

At that time, it was by synchronicities, and I knew very early on that basically it was my purpose. That's why I do what I do.

So please ask yourself the questions:

- Are you happy in your current job?
- Are you following your purpose in your career and your life?

8
Why Eight Words Are Important

The eight words are important because they say who we are. They provide a blueprint for our life.

Once you know them, they're your focus. They're your direction. They're your life and take you out of your current life and into a new one, whether painful or not.

How eight words can change your life

There's a lady I know who lived her life at ninety miles an hour. She has two young children and was constantly stressed.

Her eight words are very important to her; they are: *Focus on my drive and enjoy the journey.* Her drive gets her to such a big, high place. This idea, that idea; this change, that change; this idea, that idea.

The result was her team couldn't catch up with her. She was going ninety miles an hour and she lost people and, consequently, she got much busier and more stressed.

And was she enjoying her journey? No. Was she seeing her kids grow up? No. But she's now completely changed.

She's now walking each morning. She has calmed down and lets things go in acceptance and peace. She had the courage to change and is now spending more time with her children and really getting to know them in a deeper way. She really is a changed person.

That's an example of changing one's current life into a new one. The eight words encourage you to make a decision.

Showing your difference

If we look at my words about *care to make a difference*, they gave a uniqueness to my old accountancy business. They can also give many businesses the same uniqueness that made us different.

People knew that we were different. The stories that we gave showed our differences, and due to showing our differences, our marketing also showed that difference.

It made the sales conversion a lot easier because that's what people want. They want people who care to make a difference. So, this is a complete part of the DNA of any business.

You can feel the energy when the eight words are built into the DNA of any person or business. They flow their energy, and their energy can be huge. When you walk past someone in the street, you may feel their energy.

Increased energy through eight words

Once, I was given some divining rods, and as I walked with them towards a person or a tree, the rods crossed over in front of me. That marks the boundary of their energy.

A lady who was doing a training session with me, her energy boundary was at least four metres, whereas mine was only about two metres. She challenged us to go out into the garden and use the divining rods around trees. The energy around them was absolutely vast, even for dead ones, because they still had a job to do by festering down into the sub-strata.

So you can feel the energy of a person, and you can feel the energy of a business. When the eight words are apparent, the business grows, and the person grows. The eight words help self-confidence and self-worth. They can realign a business (this is discussed later in Chapter 9, "Decision Making"). They provide an aide-memoire for your life and can get your life back on track.

If you ever have a bad day, if you ever wonder why you've travelled the length of the country to see a client, and you're stuck in traffic on the way home, and your mind takes over, focus on your eight words.

Did you make a difference to the person you saw that day? Yes, you did. So, therefore, get out of your troubles. Get out of your moaning/anxiety. Basically, focus on what difference you made that day. That will bring you back to your higher purpose, your higher level, and this gets you back on track and makes your energy bounce back.

Your business purpose

The eight words are important in business as they form the purpose of the business. It's in your marketing.

I get frustrated with marketeers who don't ask the key question: *What is the purpose of your business?* Let me say that again. *What is the purpose of your business?* How can it stand out?

I was initially not allowed to put the word *bloody* in my marketing. Don't be afraid to put your purpose into your marketing. The marketing words will attract the right people for you at that current time: for you to learn, for you to help, for you to change their lives.

Having the right type of client

The 80:20 rule applies here. Eighty percent of clients may not be ideal for you, and the remaining twenty percent may be ideal. Those twenty percent could have a big effect on the world, have a ripple effect on the world. Who knows?

So don't be afraid to put your purpose in your marketing. All of my clients are now using it, and they're attracting the right type of clients. Not time wasters, not money grabbers.

As we all know, the lifetime of a client is limited. It may be one year, five years or ten years. If the lifetime of a client is seven years and you charge them £7,000 a year on average over those seven years, that's nearly £50,000. If your margin is 70%, that's £35,000 from one client over the next seven years. That's why you need to attract the right clients.

And that's why eight words are important in your marketing.

It is interesting when you ask a client what their ideal client is. Do they actually know, or do they just go for the money?

Don't waste your time on non-ideal clients. It's the ideal ones you want. Our criteria for ideal clients went from ten bullet points to three bullet points. The bullet points were (and are still relevant for me now):

- Do we like them?

- Can we make a difference to them in their lives?

- Can we create a story?

If we consider each of these bullet points separately:

- Liking people is important because we need a good relationship and be able to get back to the core values of CARE (described in Chapter 4, "Eight Words").

- Being able to make a difference is necessary since we have to know and be confident that we can help them change their lives.

- Obviously, the by-product of that is the story we use in marketing.

Confidence through motivation

Eight words are important because they are a driver. As described earlier (in Chapter 6, "Why Are We Here On This Earth?"), if this lady in America can fulfil her purpose, it will change the way mental health is taught in the USA and hopefully throughout the world.

What the eight words also give you is motivational. They kick you up the bottom when required. They get you out of your 'poor me' scenario and just say, 'crack on'. Have faith and crack on.

So, what you've learned from this chapter is that, above all else, the eight words are important. So important when you feel that you're not worthy.

Recently, I've been working with some ladies who are working in the male ego world. I've made them write in red lipstick on their bathroom mirror, or wherever they go first thing in the morning, the words: *I am worthy*. So when they wake up in the morning and see *I am worthy*, it sets them up for the day with a positive attitude.

That's why eight words are important. The eight words are really key and help people to have more confidence.

So believe in yourself and keep these words as your mantra.

9
Decision Making

Decision-making can change your life. It can turn around a relationship. It can help or hinder a business partner because it requires you to work together.

When I've worked with business partners, I get them to go into different rooms and write down their purpose, what they're here to do and why they're here on this earth. And when they come back together in the same room, I get them to share what their purpose is.

There's no problem having different purposes as long as there's only one purpose for the business. If not, we won't move forward until we've actually got the right purpose for the business.

This will remain a problem later on, although people having different opinions is fine in business. However, if they can't agree fundamentally on a strategic approach for the business and its purpose, that is going to cause a lot of problems.

Keeping your business aligned

The way I look at this is basically in the same way as a spine. For the digits or vertebrae of the spine, each one represents an element of the business:

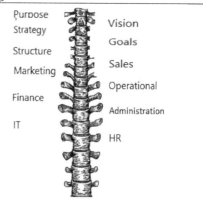

Purpose
Strategy
Structure
Marketing
Finance
IT

Vision
Goals
Sales
Operational
Administration
HR

- Purpose

- Vision

- Strategy

- Sales

- Marketing

- Operational

- Finance

- Administration

- IT

- HR

- et cetera.

If the vertebrae at the top of your spine, near your neck, goes out of alignment, it's going to make the rest of your spine out of alignment and cause you pain. If a human being has that problem, they go to a chiropractor, have an operation, undertake physiotherapy or whatever is necessary.

But where do people go to get this realigned in their business? If their purpose is not in alignment, their vision will be out of alignment. If the purpose and vision are in alignment but the strategy isn't aligned, then the rest of the business won't be in alignment. If the purpose, vision and strategy are in alignment but the sales, marketing and operations are misaligned, problems will again occur. So, in every possible way, you have to make sure your purpose is aligned with your vision.

Going back to the spine analogy, where do you go to check on your purpose? Who do you speak to? Is it a consultant, a non-executive director or your chairman? Who is it?

You can do it yourself. We have to be challenged to make sure our purpose is still in alignment. Because I really care to make a difference.

Ask yourself where you went wrong or if you had new learnings. I didn't use my eight words initially in my marketing, and I got all and sundry clients, and they weren't ideal. We invested time and effort in them, but they were just completely wrong. That is, until I made the purpose completely aligned with my vision and with the strategy and the sales and marketing. Then things started to happen.

New marketing opportunities

There's a book called *Blue Ocean Strategy* that provides marketing strategies to move from a competitive red ocean to a blue ocean with new market opportunities. The red ocean is where everybody is. If you think of it from a market perspective, all accountants are in the red ocean.

How do you get into the blue ocean? How do you be different? How do you, in Seth Godin's words, be worthy of notice? Many accountants are trying, some successfully, some unsuccessfully, to get into consultancy work and business advisory work. This is the blue ocean sector and is making them different.

A good analogy from this book is about the circus sector. There was Chipperfield's Circus and various other names that had been going on for many years. They travelled around the country with high labour and travel costs, high mileage and lengthy travelling time. On reaching each venue, they had to put up the tents and market the show. This resulted in high cost and a high level of labour although ticket prices were low.

It needed a lot of events to make a profit. Then somebody thought of Cirque du Soleil. One location, much lower labour, no clowns, no elephants, no animals whatsoever, but a performance with a high ticket price. Suddenly, they've gone from the red ocean to the blue ocean.

That's a great example of how someone has thought about a sector and made a decision to go a different way.

What creates a total difference?

Do you offer your services as board meetings? Do you offer your services as lifetime changing? Do you offer your services as a difference?

Whatever you do, you have to show and do. There's no point in talking about it. You have to do the work, and if you talk about vision, make sure you hold people accountable to their vision. If you talk about eight words, make sure you hold them accountable to their eight words. It is absolutely fundamental that these things happen and that you hold them accountable.

Do you help? Do you help create a vision for them? Do you help create a sales process that targets ideal clients?

Do you target clients that make a difference to your business by bringing in their ideal clients? Do you help create marketing words that do not use normal jargon? Do you help create a difference for the team members?

Going back a while, businesses I know used to pick up new employees from home in a limousine on their first day. They would drive them around and then get a photograph of the person with the limousine. A week later, a copy of that photograph would be sent to that person so they would always remember their first day.

That's making a difference. That's standing out.

If someone's personal goal is to go to Canada or to have orthodontic work done on their teeth, for example, and you can help them do it, they'll remember that for life. That's making a difference.

Your purpose is completely aligned, and you are making a difference everywhere in your purpose, your vision, your sales, your marketing, your teams and so on.

Everyone is ideal in your office, in your business. If anyone leaves, they leave for a good reason — they emigrate, they have a career change, or they retire. Nobody leaves because of bad will. They all grow within the business, so it is your decision to make them happy and help them grow within the business.

Focus on your purpose

Look at where differences can be made and at the story of your journey. Look at hotels and their receptionists. Do they perform what they say on their strapline? Do they actually show up and do what they say in their purpose?

I notice a lot, especially with top-class restaurants, that people receive only basic customer service. You can find out very quickly whether that is in the DNA of their business or not. For good decision-making, you create policies and systems; you create a care package.

Are you having a marriage with your clients/customers, or are you having an affair with your clients/customers? We all know the difference and how we act. Some businesses split up because they cannot agree on the purpose if their eight words are so different. It helps with finance if you are focused on your purpose and then, as a by-product, you make money.

You can have different bank accounts so that one has money to spend on marketing and another has money to spend on projects. One can be money to spend on living expenses, one for holidays, and one for tax.

You allocate pots of money from the outcome of this focus on purpose so that you can then make decisions. You will, for example, only be able to afford to go on holiday if there is enough money in the designated bank account. If there isn't, that's because you spent money elsewhere.

Similarly, with different bank accounts, you can see whether you have enough money to spend on a marketing campaign. You can tell straightaway whether you have money in any particular pot to do something. It's a very interesting concept and one that I truly believe in and practice myself.

So we can see how the eight words really help decision making by ensuring your purpose is completely aligned in the business.

10
Helping Mental Calmness and Stress (to Allow your Purpose to Flow)

"Nothing gives life more purpose than the realisation that every moment of consciousness is a precious and fragile gift" (Steven Pinker)

In May 2023, an organisation called *Wise Humanity* put out a blog entitled *Tackling Anxiety with Emotional Hygiene*. This coincided with Mental Health Awareness Week and was intended to illustrate how to deal with anxiety and challenging emotions.

A significant message is that we're not taught how to handle our inner world but are encouraged to repress our feelings and try to get on with life. But that doesn't work when we experience events that adversely affect our lives, and we need to deal with them better to achieve the best outcome.

Good and bad events

We label events, such as losing our job or separating from a partner, as bad because they seem that way at the time. But we don't know what will happen next because the event will trigger other events that may turn out well. To illustrate this, there's a famous story from Buddhism about a farmer and a neighbour.

Back in the Middle Ages, there's this farmer in a village and he wants to change his life. He has a bit of land and he wants to improve his farming. So he borrows money from all the neighbours and he buys a stallion that will help him in his work. That night, there's a big storm, the stallion gets scared and manages to run away from the stable.

The next day all the neighbours go to the farmer and say, "Oh, look at you, you wanted to change your life. Your stallion has now gone and you're destitute; you still owe us money." He shrugs his shoulders and says, "Good thing, bad thing, who knows?"

The farmer then goes for a walk in the woods to collect his thoughts and bumps into his stallion, which is eating grass with another nine wild horses. He catches them all, takes them back to the farm and builds a stronger stable. By all standards, he's now a rich man with ten horses.

All the neighbours go to the farmer and say, "Oh, look at you. We thought you were destitute, but now you're so rich and you're going to change your life and it will be great." And the farmer shrugs his shoulders and says, "Good thing, bad thing, who knows?"

The next day, the farmer and his son are taming the horses but the son falls off a horse and breaks a leg. The leg heals crooked and all the neighbours go to the farmer and say, "Oh, look at you, you had such a fine son. But now his leg is crooked and he won't be able to help you at work. He won't find a good spouse. Poor you." And the farmer shrugs his shoulders and says, "Good thing, bad thing, who knows?"

The next day, the king of that kingdom declares war on a neighbouring kingdom. All the youths need to go to war except the son of the farmer because he has a crooked leg.

So all the neighbours go to the farmer and say, "Oh, how lucky you are. Our sons went to war. We don't know if we'll ever see them again. But your son is here with you." And the farmer shrugs his shoulders and says, "Good thing, bad thing, who knows?"

This illustrates the concept of us deciding what something is before we know enough about it. In this case, we don't know whether the outcome is bad or good because it keeps changing.

According to Davide Pagnotta, Co-founder of Wise Humanity and the main contributor to this blog, events themselves are neutral, and they're only bad if we label them so. By doing so, we trigger suffering, anxiety and stress. So, instead, we should say: "Good thing, bad thing, who knows?" to each one.

Rising to the challenge

Events can be unsettling, and he believes it's okay to be unsettled: "A little adrenaline is fine. Your brain is telling your body, 'Rise to the challenge.' It keeps you awake and responsive. A little anxiety may not necessarily be something negative all the time. But you only realise that the moment you accept it. Because if you try to block it or ignore it, then you're just in this fight between your mind and something that is actually already happening."

Another source of stress, he feels, is worrying about things we can't control. That includes being too concerned about the past and the future. Instead, we should focus on the concept: **the present moment is the moment where you have power**.

There's nothing we can do about the past. Often, we're overwhelmed by a sense of responsibility and regret about something we wish we'd done differently. We are responsible for what we did or didn't do, and that's fine. But there's nothing we can do in the past, and it does no good to be stuck with regret or guilt. Instead, we need to respond positively.

There's also nothing we can do in the future until it becomes present. So we have to accept and tell ourselves we are going to handle it. This puts us in the present and empowers us so we can take action and our emotions can flow.

Davide also thinks that employers can and should help their employees if they have emotional stress and are struggling: "If I'm your boss, I can understand that you're going through this moment, and I understand that you're doing the best you can with the tools you have. So I can give you permission to go and create a moment where you feel safe, where you can give yourself a physical or metaphorical hug, relax and pause for a moment. It's fine that you're going through what you're going through.

"It's acceptance of our humanity. In the office, many times, we end up just performing actions or roles, but the human underneath is fundamental. And the more AI or technology progresses, the more important the human part is."

Controlling your emotions

If you know you're on the right path, do you need stress? Do you feel stress? You don't if you have emotional mastery.

Peace
Acceptance
Courage

Pride
Anger
Lust
Fear
Guilt
Apathy

To help you remember this, the mnemonic is AGFLAPCAP, working from bottom to top. The key is to have emotions that are above the line and avoid those that are below, especially if you are feeling stressed. Let me give you an example.

You are driving along the road, and somebody cuts you up. So what's your emotion? If it's anger, that will trigger an action from your emotion, which could be to give an abusive sign or to shout harsh words to the other driver. That will leave you feeling stressed or angry for the rest of the journey.

To counteract this, there's something called TEAR, which stands for:

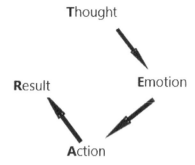

When something happens, you have a nanosecond before you **react** or **respond**.

If you react and respond correctly, you use a principle known as SOAR, which stands for:

- **S**top
- **O**bserve your emotion
- **A**ccept
- **R**elease.

This can be viewed as:

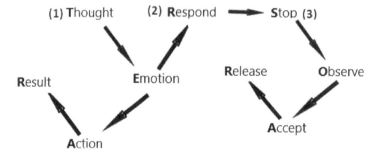

Before you become emotional, you decide to respond by going to stop. You observe your thinking, you accept your thinking, and you release on it. If you do go to emotion, action results, and you are reacting, but not usually in a good way.

Affective realism is the science behind this concept. Studies showed how emotions actually affect what we see and how we react.

Going back to the example, the other driver is going really fast and cuts you up. Instead of becoming emotional, you stop your thinking, and you observe it. You're just about to go into anger mode, but you decide to stop and instead go into acceptance mode.

You accept that the person is driving really fast and must be in a hurry. You hope he's okay. And guess what? You release, and you're at peace. So you have the courage to go into stopping, observing, accepting and releasing rather than going into anger mode and then ending it by being stressed.

When something happens, you need to go to SOAR rather than TEAR. You then get to acceptance, and you achieve peace. This is really important, and it's basically all about not having an instant reaction but instead sitting back and considering everything before you react.

You're more likely to respond in a better manner. That's because, instead of reacting in a nanosecond, you take a little longer to think about it and so you come back through in a peaceful state. So the results should be better, and you won't do something you will regret.

You have to help your mental calmness and your stress. You have to realise where your mind is taking you.

Handling daily challenges

You have two monkeys, one on each shoulder. One monkey is saying you can't do it, don't get up, you're not worthy. You can liken it to the devil and God. On the other shoulder, the monkey is saying that, of course, you can do it, have faith.

This is a challenge every day. It's a subject that's covered in the Bible quite a lot: about the devil trying to steal your thoughts, steal your purpose and steal you away from your true life. So it's really important that you realise how your mind takes you to different places.

You need to be in places where you are at peace and have acceptance and courage. So be at peace in the present moment, accept what will happen and have the courage to have faith in your eight words.

Letting energy flow

Nelson Mandela was an angry young man at one point but very vocal about what was going on. He was courageous. But did he fall into anger?

He was in fear because he was imprisoned. At what point did he go from fear to acceptance? In his book, he talks about being friendly with his jailers. He basically only had his mind to rely upon and to help him get into a good place.

I have no idea, in the 27 years he spent in jail, how many times he worried about where he was. But he then became familiar with his jailers and began to accept what he was because his energy went up. This is linked to energy.

He had the courage to accept where he was. Then that energy flowed out from where he was, and then there was all this love for him when he became a free man.

After 27 years, when he came out, he was in complete peace mode, and he loved everybody. He had such high vibration and high energy. That's really important here because, having got to peace as he did, he changed the world. He changed South Africa for the better. I know there are problems there but, even so, at that time he did huge things.

So, it's really important to notice how your energy can change by letting your mind tip you over. And that's why the eight words are important here.

Staying in the present

Being in the present moment is absolutely key. The past is the past. The future is the future. If you actually look at your mind, it's taking you to the present and the future; it's taking you to worry or to excitement, or whatever it is.

If you live in the present moment, as the author, Eckhart Tolle, talks about being in the now, then you have no worries because you're only here at this present time. There are no worries about getting home or about your journey tomorrow. No problem about the conflict meeting you have to come to. So, if you're living in the now, there is no past or future, and there is no stress.

If you come back to your eight words, if you meditate on your eight words and breathe and go to a higher place, then this will calm you down. Meditate every day for fifteen or twenty minutes.

What is meditation?

Someone once said to me that we feed our bodies with water and food, but how do we feed our minds? How do we clear our minds? How do we let our minds grow?

That is meditation. If you meditate on your eight words each day, and it takes you to a higher place and your higher purpose, then this will definitely come through and help you get to peace. So make it your mantra.

What I've learned from this is that stress can be good and bad. Who knows what good and bad are, as illustrated earlier by the story? Can stress be healthy? Can mental health be healthy? I think you need to look at the mind to see where it's taking you, and it's important to notice the difference and the having peace inside.

Using TEAR and SOAR, using your purpose, using meditation and using a mantra. Helping you get to a bigger place and helping you to be at peace is the true message of this chapter.

11
Meditation/Mantra Every Day

Meditation, as mentioned in the previous chapter, feeds the mind. You feed the body with water and food, but how do you feed the mind?

Think of it as water being murky, then the murkiness all settles to the bottom, and you have clean water to watch thoughts travel through — this is meditation.

By being quiet, having solitude, going for walks, running and speaking. Each to their own. Yoga or meditation.

A simple meditation technique

I use a simple technique known as Vipassana. It's an Indian meditation technique, which you can find on YouTube, where you sit quietly with your legs folded and spine upright for thirty minutes (or a shorter period and more regularly) and focus on your breathing. Every five minutes, a gong sounds, which is a reminder to bring you back from your mental activity, with your mind overtaking everything else, and bring you back to the present.

How do you do that? I focus on each breath. I normally have eighty to ninety breaths in the first five minutes. I focus on each breath and take my time breathing in and out. Really deep breathing in and out.

For the next five minutes, I go to forty breaths; for the next five minutes, 28 breaths, then I go down to fourteen breaths, and for the last five minutes, I let go. The lowest I've got to in five minutes is nine breaths.

You can also meditate on peace (where you are peaceful) or on joy (in all your senses).

Clearing your mind

It's very important that you find a way to reconnect with your mind and find a way to clear it in order to enable your purpose to flow. I walk for an hour or an hour and a half every day and sometimes, if I'm busy in my head, I look down and I can't remember any of the walk.

I force myself to look up and I look at the trees and at the sky, and I hear the birds. I undertake my walks, and I enjoy looking up. And now I'm aware of what's ahead because I'm not looking down, so I tell clients and myself to look up. Look up and enjoy what's around you.

When I'm looking down, I'm in the past or the future. I'm not in the present moment. If I look up, I'm in the present moment. So these simple things get you out of your head and really help.

If you run or undertake any sport, that takes you out of your head. The quietness is your meditation. People can be in solitude and be in a good space.

I took up yoga six years ago and I've just been on a yoga course in the Himalayas for ten days. When I was in the Himalayas, I was definitely between heaven and earth, doing yoga twice a day with people of the same mentality as me.

I could feel my mind clearing, and it helps that there's no signal up in the Himalayas, so there are no interruptions from phone calls, messages or emails. A wonderful experience.

If you meditate on the word joy (as mentioned above), it will always bring a smile to your face. If you focus on what joy means to you, it brings a smile to you. People were saying the Lord's Prayer and meditating on that.

> *Our Father, who art in heaven,*
> *hallowed be thy name;*
> *thy kingdom come;*
> *thy will be done;*
> *on earth as it is in heaven.*
> *Give us this day our daily bread.*
> *And forgive us our trespasses,*
> *as we forgive those who trespass against us.*
> *And lead us not into temptation;*
> *but deliver us from evil.*
> *For thine is the kingdom,*

the power and the glory,
for ever and ever.
Amen.

This is a very powerful subject for meditation because there is so much in it.

Noticing your senses

Meditating on something will bring your mind back if it wanders off. That's why the gong sounds and it's really important that you notice when your mind wanders off.

The next stage is to notice your senses:

- **Five things to hear**. Just listen to the birds, listen to the trees, listen to the wind and listen to the water; listen to anything. Listen to five things you've never appreciated before.

- **Four things to see**. Open your eyes and look at four things you've never noticed before. It can be the shape of the tree, the shade of green of the grass. It can be seeing a bird or a dog. It can be seeing anything, so look at four things you've never noticed before.

- **Three things to feel**. Feel three things. Is it the wind, the heat or the hard ground? Is it your connection to earth and trees?

- **Two things to smell**. What do you actually smell? Can you smell the newly cut grass? Can you smell anything to do with the air?

- **One thing that you taste**.

So, five, four, three, two, one for the senses. And always say your mantra: *Because I care to make a bloody difference.*

Say that and think about the ripple effect.

Being better each day

If you're walking around you may see some rubbish on the road or in the hedgerow — it could be a Coke can or a lager can, it may be plastic or anything. So pick it up because you don't know how long that's going to be there.

That one thing can make a difference so do something better each day, helping wherever you can. Pay for someone's lunch, pay for someone's car parking. Do fifty random acts of kindness each day, helping anywhere and anyone.

Make it a habit so it's in your consciousness, and before long, it becomes a part of your sub-consciousness, so you do it every day. You just do it naturally, and you'll notice when it kicks in because the eight words automatically come into flow. This is so important.

You will see a difference, and that difference may be picking up a Coke can, it may be paying someone's parking fee, or it may be letting someone out from a side road. It can be anything at all.

Who you truly are

There's human nature, and there's busyness. Never forget your human nature but just be who you truly are.

When you are in the flow of your purpose, your words help every being that you come across. A client created eight words and put them on a frame in their bedroom. That person wakes up every day and sees it in front of her bed, on the wall. Every time she wakes up, that's a great mantra.

As mentioned previously, when you're suffering with confidence or feeling unworthy or not valued, then put in big letters: *I am worthy, I am valued, I am important, I am of consequence* or something similar. Whatever the 'I am' is, write it in red lipstick on a mirror or somewhere that you see every day, in the same way as your eight words in a frame.

Make this part of your meditation; make it part of your eight words. This will really help to cleanse your mind and allow you to get to a higher energy, a higher space and higher vibration, and to be who you truly are and fulfil your purpose.

12
To Be Pure

Being pure also means being authentic. And leadership is equally important to install your purpose into your life and business. This includes leadership for yourself and for all those who look up to you.

What is leadership?

Leadership defines what the future should look like, aligns people with their purpose and vision, and inspires them to make the vision happen despite the obstacles.

Sir John Harvey-Jones said that 'Leaders should only do what only they can do.' But what exactly is that? What should you be doing as a leader?

The following topics focus on the core tasks that you should be doing as a leader.

The core tasks that belong to a leader

These are the things that you MUST do as a leader.

1. Define your purpose and values and live by them.
2. Establish direction.
3. Decide on strategy.
4. Build an unstoppable team.
5. Set up systems to feed back key information.
6. Drive the business forward.

Each of these tasks will now be explored in further detail.

Define your values and live by them

As a leader, you must be the person who creates the right culture within your business.

Jim Collins and Jerry I. Porras found that one of the fundamental elements in the visionary companies they studied was what they called a core ideology: the core values and a sense of purpose that guide and inspire people throughout the organisation.

The core values are the organisation's essential and enduring tenets — a small set of guiding principles.

The core purpose is the organisation's fundamental reason for existence beyond just making money. It is not to be confused with specific goals or business strategies, which change over time. The core purpose should not change, although it should inspire change. For example, the core purpose of Walt Disney is 'to make people happy'.

The core purpose has a key role in guiding and inspiring. It goes beyond just making money because this does not inspire people at all levels of the organisation, and it does not provide much guidance.

So, what is your core ideology?

There is no right or wrong core ideology; it is what you believe is your purpose. In the visionary companies, Jim Collins and Jerry Porras found that no single item showed up consistently. For some companies, their customers were central to their ideology. To others, it was their team; to others, their products or services. Or risk-taking. Or innovation.

They found that it was the authenticity of the ideology (purpose) and the extent to which a company attains consistent alignment with the ideology that counted more than the content. And they found that the very act of stating a core ideology influences behaviour toward consistency with that ideology.

And as a result of stating their core ideology, the visionary companies more thoroughly indoctrinated their team into it, more carefully nurtured and selected senior management based on their fit with it, and more consistently aligned their goals, strategies, tactics and organisational design.

By influencing behaviour, stating a core ideology will impact the culture within your practice. And since many challenges within most of the practices we come across stem from a bad culture, then working on your core ideology is a great starting point in developing the right culture for your business.

However, if your core ideology (purpose) is not passionately held on a gut level, then it is not core. It needs to be meaningful and inspirational to you and your team (hence the eight words).

Creating an authentic business

How often do you come across a truly authentic business? Their employees are complete ambassadors of authenticity. If you take easyJet, for example, are their employees a true reflection of their brand? Most of them are very polite and very helpful, but if you go to a different chain such as WH Smith, are the people there reflective of their brand? (This implies nothing against WH Smith!)

What is their brand? Many people don't know, so you need to make sure your brand is pure and authentic. What does pure stand for? In my words:

- **P**erfect
- **U**tterances
- **R**emaining
- **E**thical.

Pure is the keyword here. You will go off track, you will sin, and you will be forgiven. Your eight words bring you back, so learn and come back to your eight words. Say your eight words on a daily basis.

Divine wisdom = purity = being authentic.

Always being authentic

Authentic means to say and do and follow through and to have gratitude for what this means.

There's an example where somebody was going to buy into a business and repeated constantly that it was going to happen, that he would pay £50,000 for 5% of the business. The business was purchased, but the person who had promised to invest then backed out. He wasn't authentic because he didn't fully follow through.

A client of mine has taught all forms of yoga for ten or twelve years now. But suddenly, she's saying that yoga's become too commercial, too buzzwordy and therefore, it's become unauthentic. What she's seeing is courses to teach yoga in six or nine months.

She teaches yoga for over eighteen months, over 300 hours. It's vitally important that you take time for the teachings to sink in rather than rush it and not be an authentic yoga teacher. I'm not saying that six months or nine months is wrong, but I think my client's got it right and really allows people to accept it and be authentic in their learnings.

As a further example, recently I went to see a football game between Real Mallorca and Valencia. After the game, we went down to a bar where the players came in. One of them was a 22-year old footballer who played all the game and played well.

There must have been about thirty women from the same country who were looking at him when he came through the door. He looked up and he must have been frightened in some way because he just stood there, didn't look at them and didn't acknowledge them but looked at his phone for a few minutes and then walked off. He didn't even say hello to any of them.

When we drove out of the car park, there were fans on the left, right and in front of the exit. There must have been over 200 fans there. There were rumours he was going to play for a Premiership team (although he's since moved to Paris Saint-Germain in France), but he was completely unauthentic and frightened at that moment, and I hope his bosses show him how to be a true, authentic person because those people travelled a long way to see him.

There's often a complete disjoint between the fans and the people they support, although they're not all like this because some genuinely like their fans. I did, for instance, see a post recently about a player who was responding to fans in the early hours of the morning, which shows he's truly authentic about what he's trying to achieve.

So where does the disjoint happen? Again, I come back to the point about care.

Caring and listening

A lot of businesses in this country have the word care on their websites. But what does it actually mean? How do they care for their clients? How do they care for the team members? There are plenty of examples where they may say one thing but do another and don't follow through, and they get found out as a leader.

That's why the important points about being a leader and being authentic in the early part of the chapter are totally correct. How would you be authentic with clients? You can tell.

If someone is listening:

- they're making eye contact
- they're not thinking about their next question
- they are being empathetic
- they sit there and wait for a pause rather than interrupting and then ask the right question.

So that is true listening. We have one mouth and two ears, so we use both ears.

Then, it comes to how an employee actually values their leader.

In these current times, people are constantly being headhunted. If they're going for the money, then they'll go, and you probably can't stop them.

Is it possible to gain any loyalty now? I believe it is, but how?

By showing that you care. If there is a work anniversary, whether one, five or ten years, celebrate it. If there's been an achievement, celebrate it.

If someone has done something great, celebrate it. If they've not done something so great, don't give them a hard time. Instead, just let them know that they're learning and it's okay to fail and learn.

These are different examples of caring for employees, but mostly, it's about being there and being present. It's often the small things that matter and are most memorable.

Building Authentic Relationships

That leads to your authenticity if this then is mirrored in your relationship with your clients. Again, it's the difference between marriage and an affair. Marriage is long-term; it's a journey. Sometimes, it's hard work, but it's a partnership, and therefore, it's really important that you work on a relationship.

An affair is unauthentic. We all know what goes on in an affair, and therefore, you need to decide whether you have a marriage or an affair with your clients.

David Maister has written several business books, including one called *True Professionalism*. This was back in the late nineties, and there's a chapter on having a marriage or an affair with clients.

Authenticity is absolutely key and being pure as well in all your dealings. If you find yourself being unauthentic, just be aware of it. Don't give yourself a hard time, but change your habits. Make sure your consciousness and subconsciousness kick in so that you are authentic and pure in all that you do.

Your energy will radiate even more, and the light will spread. And that's the biggest learning of this chapter.

Relationships will remain and blossom.

13
Core Ideology/Purpose

"The light burning within you is a far more accurate reflection of who you are than the stories you've been telling yourself."
(B Grace Bullock)

You communicate by your energy, your vibrations and your higher self. Who do you communicate your eight words to and share with? Trust family and friends, business relationships and all types.

In a previous chapter, I explained how you get your eight words and your purpose. It's important you share those eight words with trusted people, people who don't scoff at them, people who don't sap your energy. People who are naysayers.

Choose people who have the same vibration as you and use them for their great feedback. The lady described in Chapter 5, who performs medicine ceremonies, shared the words on her Facebook page, and the comments she received were fantastic. There were over a hundred comments on her Facebook page simply from sharing her purpose and there is no doubt that will lead to her fulfilling her purpose.

When you communicate your eight words, how does it happen?

Communicating in the Right Way

Many years ago on television, there was a man called David Icke, a sports presenter, who claimed to be a 'Son of the God' and predicted that the world would soon be devastated by tidal waves and earthquakes. He went on TV in his purple shell suit, and he was widely ridiculed and treated as a fool. But, actually, some of the things he said were quite right in certain aspects, but his presentation at that time wasn't appropriate.

As well as television, do you communicate in talks and speeches? Do you get on stage? Do you write in papers? Do you do it in books? I'm trying here to communicate my purpose in this book, as many people have done previously.

People write songs. There is a four-day medicine festival with music in Newbury, England, every year. All the performers have written songs about Mother Earth, about the sky, the clouds, about trees, about spirit and about plant-based medicines to help. It's a truly magical ceremony.

That has a ripple effect on those people who attend the festival and share their experiences. It's all within the lyrics, and those lyrics come from spreading the belief that true medicine comes from authentic plants that can help you get out of your true self.

Some people write poems. There's a poem I wrote in the Himalayas, which is vitally important to me because it was in a place where I sat with about twenty-five mountain peaks in front of me. This poem is in the Preface to this book and I've shared it with many people who say they like it and I should publish it, so there it is.

Being up in the Himalayas gave me inspiration, so writing the poem took only twenty-five minutes. I've never written a poem before in my life and it was truly unbelievable. So you can communicate with poems and they are truly a way of doing it.

You can do it in papers, as mentioned earlier, but you must make sure you use authentic language. And that's true for all language that you use.

The importance of sharing your eight words

"Not everything that is faced can be changed, but nothing can be changed until it is faced" (James Baldwin)

When you share your eight words with friends, get them to challenge you, help you, support you, inspire and motivate you. It's up to you whether you use family or not because sometimes you can separate your purpose from the family.

One lady created her eight words and she shared them with her sons and daughter. She found it amazing what came up and she was truly inspired by creating the eight words herself with her sons and daughter.

I mentioned in Chapter 6 the lady in New York who's created a book with the aim of changing the way mental health is taught in America.

She wants to change the way eleven to eighteen-year-olds are affected by this, and the impact of the book and everything connected to it has been absolutely huge.

To communicate, we go to marketing. The eight words should be in every marketing medium. They should be on your social media, on your website, and on your letterhead. If you provide your eight words, then don't hide them.

For business partners, share your eight words and see if you can work together. It's all about communication, so talk to managers, share your eight words and see if you can work together and get feedback. Share with your employees, ask them about your eight words and get their feedback.

Authentically communicate and get feedback. In the same way, as your vertebrae need to be aligned along your spine, align your eight words with the business and all stakeholders. Understand what they are and why.

Take an honest look at yourself

As a leader, you must take personal responsibility for everything that is not right about your business. You must communicate effectively with your employees.

Does your team feel inspired? Do they feel part of a team that knows where it is going? Do they buy into your purpose and vision for the business and understand the strategy for achieving that vision? Do they find you are a good decision-maker? Do people feel they are given enough information, or do they think you keep them in the dark? Do they have confidence that you will do what you say you will do? Do your managers believe that you delegate enough to them and allow them to get on with their job?

Answer these questions honestly.

And if something is not right in your business, then it is a sign that there is something that you've got to learn. Something that you've got to change. And that may need to start with a change within you. Michael Gerber tells us that our business is a mirror of us. If our business is disorganised it is because we are disorganised. If our people are angry, it is because we are making them angry.

Until leaders admit that they make mistakes, they cannot be truly effective. One of the most important steps on the way to being a great leader is to ensure that you learn every day and are humble. The key is to admit to yourself that, however many years you've been in business, you don't know everything, and you can always learn and improve.

So, you need to strive constantly to become a better leader.

14

To Have a Culture Ethos in Business

"Before you speak, let your words pass through three gates.
At the first gate, ask yourself, 'Is it true?'
At the second gate, ask yourself, 'Is it necessary?'
At the third gate, ask yourself 'Is it kind?" (Rumi)

Core values are the principle of every business. It's essential you make sure everything has a structure around it and that you get team buy-in.

If you have a team day, make sure you put your own values out there linked to your purpose and then ask the team to challenge those values to see whether they believe in them. That's absolutely key.

Adopting core values

Core values are to have a culture ethos everywhere in the business. Core values must be prevalent.

At Clear Vision, we had the following value statement that incorporates our core value of care:

Culture

- Be positive
- Have a supportive, fun-filled environment
- If you have a problem with someone, talk about the problem with them face-to-face
- Apologise and make good if someone is upset by your actions
- Blame a system, not a person
- When you talk about someone who is not present, speak as if they are listening to your conversation
- Treat each other with respect
- Ensure that no question ever arises about our ethics

Attitude

- Bring your best attitude to work
- Be the best you can at all times
- Push yourself to develop and learn

Relationship

- Make sure those who work with us can testify to learning a lot, having a great experience and enjoying a fantastic relationship
- Work with great people who value, inspire and want to develop us, from whom we can learn and who we enjoy associating with
- Grow via innovative, high-quality services and the acquisition of like-minded clients

Excellence

- Do exceptional work and be known for it
- Constantly question the way things are done in order to constantly improve service
- Dot the 'i's' and cross the 't's' and never forget that excellence is in the detail.

What are core values?

Core values are principles or beliefs that a person or organisation views as being of central importance. This applies to employees of a company as well as the company itself. It's absolutely key that there's a belief of central importance. That's why we get people to go through this process.

Core values drive behaviour and form beliefs. For example:

- Reliability
- Dependability
- Loyalty
- Honesty
- Commitment
- Consistency
- Efficiency.

People who are in satisfying or great relationships will often say their partner shares their values. Where there is a misalignment of values, there are break-ups.

Human values are:

- Respect
- Acceptance
- Consideration
- Appreciation
- Listening
- Openness
- Affection
- Love towards other human beings.

Making core values part of the ethos of your business

Somebody I know has three core values in the business:

- **Trust** that what is stated will actually be done.
- **Excellence** in all that is done within the team, within the business and with all clients.
- **Candid** by being frank and impartial, upfront and truthful in everything that's said.

An accountancy firm I know has Support, Inspire and Challenge. Consequently, at every meeting, these values are discussed — Are we supporting you? Are we inspiring you? Are we challenging you?

Team members know that's what they have to do in every meeting, and that's the ethos of the business. It's on their strap line, on their website and on everywhere. It's what they do, and it's actually part of their eight words.

Many times, core values are only eight words and so they should be; it's no surprise that they are.

Using core values to uphold purpose

For divine wisdom and eight words, the purpose needs upholding, and part of the way this is done is by using core values. Seeing and showing it as the ethos of the business. Speak examples of core values; speak as though somebody else is in the room.

Treat suppliers and customers with respect. Determine whether a client is ideal or not (described earlier in Chapter 8, "Why Eight Words Are Important") and make sure honesty is at the core of everything. Make sure excellence is in everything that you do. Ensure you are a better person today than you were yesterday. Strive and grow.

In hotels, sometimes there are core values displayed behind the reception desk. Some of those words are truly important and are the branding of the business. But, if the receptionists don't deliver those core values, there is a complete disjoint. There is incongruousness, and therefore, the core values are breached.

Other businesses put core values on the wall in their meeting rooms, in the main operations rooms, on their website, on their headed paper and have them signed off by the whole firm.

The core values are key. If you consider the eight words being in the centre of a circle and core values being a supporting circle, then that's absolutely key as well. As is making sure there are systems around those concentric circles.

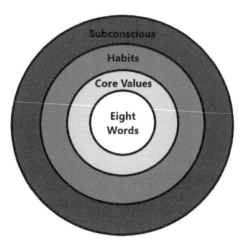

If you use this model, you'll truly make core values part of the DNA of your business (described in the next chapter).

Core values have been important to me and have also helped the team follow values. I didn't mind being challenged on them or, indeed, individuals being challenged on them as they should be. By doing this, you find out whether people are aligned with your business and should actually be in your business or not.

15

To Make Eight Words the DNA of the Business

DNA is a molecule that carries genetic information for the development and functioning of an organism. It's in the form of a double helix, a helix being a three-dimensional shape like that of a wire wound uniformly in a single layer around a cylinder or cone.

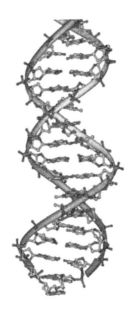

This DNA symbol ironically incorporates the eight we use in our eight words and, when turned on its side, can be seen to represent infinity. It also has body shapes in there.

Aligning DNA with your business

DNA is wrapped around the eight-word purpose:

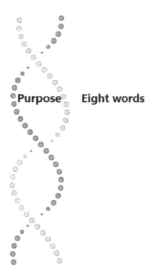

DNA is likened to the imagery of the word purpose, and there are a few eights in there that are all intertwined. So, the DNA and the specifics of purpose and vision align your business.

DNA is within everything you do: the people, the clients you attract, the language you use, the care you show and the people who stay with you. It shows that you are authentic, that you are real, that they trust you, that they want you to be on their journey and you learn from it and grow, and they grow with you. They then carry some of that DNA to other places, and it spreads.

That DNA is absolutely crucial to be part of the business and it's an important element when determining your business strategy.

Decide on strategy after your purpose is defined

Strategy provides both logic and a first level of detail to show how a vision can be accomplished.

Although there are many definitions of strategy, a simple but effective definition is '*Considering the alternative ways of getting to point B*'.

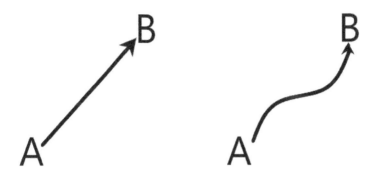

Point B is where you want to be in the future – your vision. And, inevitably, there will be more than one way of getting there. You need to consider all of those routes and then choose the best one.

John P. Kotter provides us with a useful illustration of where strategy fits with vision, the role of a leader and management.

The relationship of vision, strategies, plans and budgets

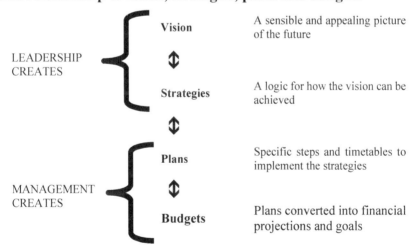

Source: "Leading Change", John P Kotter

Once vision, values and strategy have been defined, the rest of your business plan will flow from that.

Creating the right systems

When you have a strategy, from that, you can create a structure. Then, from the structure and the strategy, you develop your profile, your sector and your clients. You develop your marketing, the language and attraction.

You look at the functioning of your operations, your core values and your personal process. You look at the functionality of your human resources systems and ensure they are the best. Similarly, assess the function of your IT systems to make sure they are as efficient as possible and look at the function of your financial systems and administration systems to see if they are delivering everything linked to the DNA.

It's all about systems and core values. The DNA is everything that you do, and it's part of the key message of the business. I've already said that, in the eight words, you need core values wrapped around them. You also need to enforce the DNA of your business.

So, who is the enforcer of the DNA? Is it the Managing Director, the Chief Executive Officer or the Operations Director? Is it the whole team?

It needs to be the accountability of the whole team and there's an example of how we do that in the next chapter. What I mean by enforcing DNA is if, in the example of my words, it's about the difference, how do you know your team is making a difference?

The way we did it is we had a big whiteboard. Every Monday morning, everybody, without fail, had to give one example of how they had made a difference to a client the previous week. We put that on the whiteboard, and we shared it. We created momentum around that.

Even though they were only helping a client to submit a tax return or to help on a financial query, they were still making a difference. They were still solving a problem and providing a solution. Sometimes, we take for granted what we do as part of the process, but we should celebrate the fact that we are doing this within the DNA of our business.

When there is a mutation in the DNA, when there's something missing, such as a chromosome, there's something in your body that affects you. Albinos, for example, have mutations in certain genes, and DNA doesn't change because it can't change.

Respecting your DNA in the business

If you don't treat your 'DNA' with respect, then your mind becomes unhealthy, your body becomes unhealthy, the team becomes unhealthy, the whole business becomes unhealthy, and you start losing people.

A manufacturing business I know had a change of leadership ten years ago, and, at the time, there were twenty-five people working there. Within two and a half years, the new owners lost nine of the key people due to the change of leadership. This led to a change of core values and the employees not believing in the leader.

Losing those key people meant the company had to use expensive recruitment agencies, retrain and refocus. So it cost a lot of money and lost productivity, all because of the change of core values and the change in the DNA. It's absolutely crucial people realise this and don't change the DNA of the business.

The Scandinavian airline SAS was in financial trouble and brought in a new CEO to sort things out. The CEO asked 'what are the three key functions of the business?'

The key DNA of the business was to get the planes to arrive on time, to get the luggage arriving on time and to make sure there's no lost luggage. Those three things were focused on and were the three key factors.

Any stewardess or steward who was asked knew what the three measurements were, and they became part of the DNA of their business. Because they focused on those three things, and they were all linked to passenger care and service, the business grew and became very successful.

So the learnings from this are to make sure you absolutely enforce the DNA of your business — the eight words, the core values, the systems, the accountability and the measurements. And make sure that you have an enforcer who does not enforce in a negative way but upholds everything, helping your team to grow and making sure they are intrinsic to your business.

16
To Sign a Charter

We've considered the DNA of the business and how it's enforced. But you also need to get accountability from the team, and you do that by getting them to sign a charter.

That charter has the eight words at the top and covers the purpose, every core value of the business and every DNA of the business. You need to discuss this with the team members and get their buy-in.

Once they've challenged you on it — which is good — on your eight words and your core values, get it all written down on a sheet of A4 paper. Then, make every employee sign that charter and date it.

Dealing with problems

If ever you get any problems going forward with any employee, all you need do is put the signed copy of the charter in front of the team member and ask them to say what's happened, how this has breached the eight words, the DNA and the core values of the business.

Then you don't need to say another word. Just let them talk, and before long, they'll talk themselves into what has gone wrong, and all you've got to say is, 'so what have you learned from this?'

It then comes down to how they are going to change their habits. So put the charter in front of them, ask them what they feel about what's happened and talk about their learnings and how to change their habits.

There's a famous film called *Meet the Fockers,* and in it, there was something called the Circle of Trust. One of the characters, Jack Byrnes, who was ex-CIA, had a situation where his future son-in-law was not in the circle of trust, and he told him so. The circle of trust comprised his wife and daughter, and he kept saying that.

At the end of the film, the son-in-law became a circle of trust member, and that was what mattered. So that was his charter.

Customer and supplier charters

Customers definitely have a charter. If you don't do what you say you're going to do, then you will lose your customer base. That's a charter in itself.

For example, for companies supplying vegetables to supermarkets, carrots had to be straight and clean, and so they are grown to that specification. If they do conform, suppliers keep their contracts and there are regular audits and checks to ensure compliance.

All suppliers have to sign a charter and adhere to it. But, in the case of carrots in particular, that led to a lot of waste for those that were not straight. So, the bent carrots are now being sold as part of a 'wonky vegetable' line to avoid waste. But, in this situation, supermarkets rule the roost.

Different charters

In teams, there are staff handbooks, employment contracts and other contracts and documents that are necessary for employment law. Then, you've got the core value charter. An example is shown next:

I am committed to continuous improvement in the areas that matter to the business, its customers and the team...

And in particular I am committed to helping the firm to achieve its vision and to meet the criteria for excellence.

There's the eight word purpose charter to you and to other people. It signs other people up to you, and they are trusted individuals.

Everything you need is already inside you. So don't hide, don't be fearful. Everyone can sign the charter and you should use it daily, weekly, for team meetings and whenever it is required.

Make sure there is an enforcer who needs this charter to do his or her job. Help them to do their job by getting this charter prepared and creating a workshop to discuss it and make sure it's completed in the appropriate way. Do this in a free space away from work with a resourcer to make sure it flows in a positive way.

17
To Be Inspired

"Let go of the old stories you tell yourself in order to make way for new ones."

Is this your chosen path? Is this God's direction for you?

The meaning of being inspired is the process of being mentally stimulated to do or feel something, especially to do something over time.

This is your bigger picture. Have no fear. What is it?

Be inspired to change your life

I was asked to give my eight words many years ago, and when I said them, I felt inspired and I felt motivated. Then, from those words, I created this different business.

From there, many people have, in their eight words, been inspired to change their lives. The lady who has the frame in front of her in the bedroom with her eight words has changed her life.

What are you inspired by? Is it to trek the Himalayas? Is it to practise dentistry? Is it to have three or four business sites? Is it to run a retreat? Is it to turn accounting businesses into consultancy businesses? Is it to write a book? What's your passion? Is it to meditate and teach meditation?

Eight words are everywhere. You need a team that wants to be led and will follow you.

Are you inspired by spiritual growth? Eight words are the start, and whatever age you are, it does not matter.

Are you enhancing your existing life? Are you starting a new life? Are you getting rid of the old life?

It's your decision and you'll be directed by God, the universe, and it will be the journey for you. It is a massive opportunity. You need to be different. You need to get rid of the old mental patterns. You need to look at your legacy, your difference. Is it going to be a start-up?

Inspiring quotations

There are several quotations that may help you.

Mahatma Gandhi said, "The best way to find yourself is to lose yourself in the service of others."

So what does that mean? It's basically saying that to find yourself, you need to lose yourself in servicing people, helping your family, servicing clients, suppliers and anyone else. Lose yourself in doing that, and it will be inspiring to all those who follow. You will definitely be in flow.

Gandhi also said: "You must be the change you wish to see in the world."

Nelson Mandela said, "What counts in life is not the mere fact that we have lived. It is what difference we have made to the lives of others."

Martin Luther King said, "We must come to see that the end we seek is a society at peace with itself, a society that can live with its conscience."

Tom Peters said, "Excellence is in the next five minutes. Or it is nothing at all." But what does that mean? Basically, what he's saying relates to what Seth Godin said about being worthy of notice.

Are you worthy of notice in your marketing? It's really important that whatever you say or do in the next five minutes, however you communicate with your client in the next five minutes, it will be seen as what excellence is.

Be inspired and inspiring

There are people in dentistry who I work with, and they have taught their team members to be in a better place to grow. The leaders have led by example and have been inspiring.

If you get a leader to talk and their voice is monotone, they won't be inspirational. However, if that leader talks from the heart with passion, that is inspiring because they get into the flow, and their passion comes through.

Only yesterday, I asked the Managing Director of a business to talk from the heart with passion about whether the business should be sold or not and it flowed really well. She gave a great presentation, and she had to do it to get it off her chest, and it was very inspiring.

To be inspired and to be inspiring are different elements. Inspiring comes from the leadership, from the top. To be inspired is from the people above you and the eight words and the purpose. As mentioned earlier, everything you need is within yourself, so you find your own inspiration within yourself.

I have my own five inspirations:

- I want to get these eight words out as much as possible and help find people's purpose. That's my key inspiration and the aim of this book.
- I want to help run a retreat in the future.
- I want to help accounting firms to deliver consultancy business to change people's lives.
- I want to help certain individuals to grow their business.
- I want to really look at training around spiritual connections and channellings.

Those are my inspirations that link to my eight words. 'Because I care to make a bloody difference' is still there for all those five things.

18
Examples and Measurements of Eight Words and Purpose

"Letting go a little brings a little peace.
Letting go a lot brings a lot of peace.
Letting go completely brings complete peace." (Ajahn Chah)

There are examples of the eight words or more that various people and organisations have developed over the years and which set out their purpose. For each, there's a description of how they measure their performance against those eight words to establish how successful they are in achieving their purpose.

It's really important that you have measurements within your eight words. I've said many times about care, how we measure care and how we measure the difference in our own eight words. If you don't measure the difference, you don't know how effective your eight words are.

The lady described earlier, who performs ceremonies, wants to do twenty of them each year. It's her vision. She wants to help over one hundred people in each ceremony or up to ten people in each private ceremony. That's her vision.

So the aim is to set a specific target and then to measure if she achieves it. In her measurement, she wants to heal, reconnect and expand people's lives.

So, how do we measure that? She normally performs ceremonies over the weekend. Did she ask for feedback? No. Did she ask people to tell a story of before and after? No. That's all changed.

We are now measuring before — how they're feeling —and after — how they're feeling. Then we can see whether this lady has really helped them to change via her purpose.

Those stories we are capturing are then used in her marketing, and that marketing will then get more clients. So it's a self-propelling wheel.

1. Focus on my drive and enjoy the journey

Measurement is time spent with family and less on projects.

2. Use your unique set of skills to transform lives

Measurement is people before and after, and any other transformations.

3. To change the way mental health is taught in the U S A

Measurements include the number of suicides in schools, a reduction of mental health issues in schools, how many schools are going to participate in the programme, the number of teachers that are going to be trained and how many people are going to go for the programme.

4. To humanise the numbers in accountancy practices

Ensure all services are linked to a change for the client in their personal and business lives.

5. To inspire, challenge and support

One particular business needs to measure how it is inspiring its team, its clients and its clients' customers. How does it challenge the team? How does it challenge the clients at every meeting?

How does it support the team, both personally and professionally? How does it support the clients in their business for measurement for all of these things in this particular business? To do this, they had what's called a 'One Page Plan'. An example of this is shown in Appendix A.

This particular business has measurements for inspiring, challenging and supporting, and every conversation was about how to inspire, challenge and support the team or the client and their customers.

6. To build a caring community and connect trees to people

In the tree world, there are a lot of male egos. Do they care about their own ego? Yes. Do they care about the trees? Yes. Is there a caring community to support all the trees? No.

So therefore, the caring community is dealing with a male ego in this particular instance. The challenge is to come together to see how they can help the tree world caring community, to actually go into schools and teach them how trees work, to help them plant trees, to get them to come out and actually care for the trees and the world and to connect trees to people.

So how can we do that? A lady is going to be spending days in National Trust locations where she'll guide students through the forests and talk about the stages the trees are at, what type of trees they are, whether they have disease or not, and how to cut them. So the students will connect and they will inform people how to connect to trees.

7. I do what I set out to do

A score is kept on the number of tasks completed each week.

8. Lead communities to change the earth

The measurement here is the number of communities, environmental, charitable, whichever ones the lady who is involved with this wants to work with. She was working in an industry where the purpose was definitely clouded and the value changed but she learned a lot in this business, specifically leadership, management and project roles.

She wants to put that skill and experience into communities around the world — environmental projects and charity projects. So she will be measuring the communities as to where she's going to lead them — the number of communities and how she's going to change the area from whatever situation it's in.

9. Help people break free from conditions

The measurement is the number of projects, and the number of people helped.

10. To really change what you want to see in the world

Measure your voice through the number of talks, podcasts and books.

11. When you cannot afford to fail

This is an explosive business that manufactures projectiles that are shot into landmines so that people don't lose their lives. So their phrase is 'when you cannot afford to fail'.

Their measurement is that every time a projectile goes off, it's saving lives and injury. Their record is a hundred percent when they use their projectiles. So their measurement is based on a negative when it doesn't work and then what they can do about it to put it right.

12. To create a doorway and a safe space for our human heart to heal and reconnect

Measurement is how people feel before and after so that improvements can be assessed. (See more detail at the start of this chapter).

13. Inspire to celebrate and expand our true, authentic self

Measurement is also of before and after feelings in order to determine the level of success.

14. Because I care to make a bloody difference

The number of people helped per day and per week.

15. To allow myself to care to provide for others

The lady who is involved here lost her mum at a very early age, and it inspired her to run her own business at the age of 32. The business collects rags from textile banks and sells them to the Middle East and Africa, and it is definitely providing for others.

She's selling to businesses that then sell to other people who sell to others. So all along, families have been provided for, and she's also caring for herself, so she's measuring that as well as the number of families. Measurements here are how many textile bundles are going out per month and how many people she's reaching in those different countries.

16. Nurturing approachable team builder who wants to solve problems

One accounting firm solves problems every day for clients. For the person who runs it, it's his forte, it's his reason for being, it's sort of his raison d'etre and he loves doing it. He has been so busy, but he's worked hard to ensure members of his team can approach him and also he nurtures them.

He's measuring how he nurtures them, measuring how technical solutions are approached, and obviously, he's building a team at the same time.

17. Enjoy life, spread positivity and make a difference

This person has a great personality, and she laughs every day. When she allows herself to come out of her head, she enjoys life even more, and she spreads positivity with her team and makes a difference. This is a simple measurement: she basically measures every day when she's made a difference.

18. Encourage people to enjoy themselves and be the best people they can be

The amount of training is measured as well as the outcomes from it.

19. Significantly help others, especially those experiencing disadvantage

This person works in a school, and there is a set of core values within that school about helping children to learn and grow. That includes those who experience disadvantage, whether it's due to race, disability, gender or anything else.

He's measuring each month how he's helping others, especially those who experience disadvantages and also the project that he's doing to help achieve these words.

20. To alchemise dark into light, leading the way into divine union into oneness

A lady guru who is helping so many people into the light measures the number of events and the people helped.

21. To inspire/to challenge to empower, enabling choice for a better lifestyle

Accountants who are helping their clients achieve a better lifestyle. Each one adopts measurements that they consider appropriate.

---

22. To provide brave spaces for people to transform and heal

This lady runs a yoga business and every space she provides, whether it's in-house or external, is pure and full of energy to allow her to do her work. Her purpose is to allow people to transform and heal. In her marketing and in her yoga classes, there is a transformation in this healing. We just need to get a measurement in place, so this is a work in progress.

23. To make the lives of strangers meaningful

The aim is to help every stranger they come across in any way they can, whether it's shopping, going to the park, team building, clients or people that they meet. It's a simple measurement because it's just a count of people helped every day.

24. Embody authentic creative living, offering compassion and correction to others, helping people to realise they are enough

Everyone you come across, build them up, make them feel confident, and make them happy. You realise they're enough and so keep saying they're enough to make sure they feel worthy. That can be measured every day.

25. To listen to vulnerable children, helping them have a voice to change their lives

This is a lovely lady who is a solicitor and works in the family division, so she deals with people in care or in divorce situations. She's so empathetic and compassionate, listening to the children to see what they want rather than what the parents want. She tries her best to ensure the children are heard and that their wishes are followed and not necessarily those of the parents.

She'll work for the benefit of the children, so it's an easy measurement. How many times do you listen each day or each week? They're normally all vulnerable children, so how many times do they have a voice, and how many times do they change their lives?

What a wonderful purpose.

Other measurements

There are many people with mental health problems, so for the lady in America described previously, her measurement is how many schools she's going to get to participate in her programme. How many teachers she's going to train, and how many people are going to go for the programme.

That's a massive opportunity to measure there and to help change people's lives. A man is measuring before and after because people have lost themselves in their own world, and therefore, he's looking to measure before, during, and after.

The lady who focuses on her drive is making sure that she goes from ninety miles an hour down to fifty miles an hour and, at the present moment, is smiling and enjoying her life. Another man is measuring his unique set of skills in practising dentistry and measuring the transformation of lives.

All of these can be measured and it's a simple measurement.

We used to measure the difference we made and put that on the website. We used to measure the stories we'd created and the effects we had on people. Accountants measure how they're humanising the numbers for their clients.

People measure how they support other people, how they inspire people, and how they challenge people. So they're all measurements.

The measurement process

Measurement is a very simple process requiring only one sheet of paper. You put your eight words and your purpose on there, you underline the words you wish to measure and you have a simple measurement programme.

That can be weekly, monthly, quarterly or six monthly, whatever you wish. But make sure you measure it.

In Chapter 1, "Divine — Step 1 to Achieving your Purpose", I talked about going from A to B and not being a straight line; indeed, it's a wavy line. In order to get to and achieve your purpose, you need to measure it and therefore, that's how you get from A to B. That's absolutely crucial.

Make sure you come out of your head, and if it's a challenging day, don't make it about the money. Make it about the purpose.

Measure where you've made a difference that day and truly reflect on that and even meditate on it. If you meditate on the measurements and how you've put them in place for people, that will raise you to your higher self rather than drop you into a low-vibration drama.

It's important you focus on that and get yourself out of yourself. That's the main message in this chapter.

Eight words can change your life

From these examples, people have changed their lives. They've enhanced their existing life, they've started a new life or have got rid of their old life. And these eight words have really driven them to be inspiring as a leader and to get to a place where they are high energy, high vibration and helping so many people.

It's a privilege to see how they fly.

19
Summary

"Yesterday is history.
Tomorrow is a mystery.
But today is a gift.
That's why they call it the present." (Unknown)

Thank you for the journey to the Himalayas and to a solitary retreat in Scotland, which are the inspirations that led me to write the poem featured in the Preface to this book and the one at the back of the book.

Thank you for life as a whole and the learnings and the mistakes that lead to even higher vibration to help people. And thank you to Jeff Senior who has helped me write this book.

Keep your purpose in alignment

Please use your eight words to find who you truly are and your true, authentic self. But always remember that if your purpose is out of alignment, you are out of alignment. You're not going in the same direction as your purpose, and you will be unhappy and unfulfilled.

If people are like that, it's no problem at all. It's their life, and they can choose what they want to do.

But it's best to put your purpose back in alignment. Follow every step of your process to make sure everything is aligned and put it into your communications. Be inspiring. Be sharing. Make sure divinity is at its heart, and make sure you share your wisdom and your knowledge.

Everyone, I believe, has a purpose that sets out from the divine, and we are challenged to fulfil this.

I encourage you to mark your life as significant and be faithful to fulfil the purpose that God has designed for you.

I hope reading this book has made a difference to you.

All those clients who over the years I have worked with on their eight words, they are on their journey.

In my eight words, I've definitely cared.

So get out there and find and do your own purpose and let's make the ripple effect help change the world to a better place.

What do you need to walk away from so that you can accomplish your plan and the purpose that is planned for you? Never be discouraged and embrace the season, and wait patiently for God's divine purpose to be revealed.

As a final word, here's a useful article from *The UCB Word for Today* website:

Start living on purpose

7 November 2023

"Those who help others are helped."

Proverbs 11:25 MSG

One of the best ways to keep your life in balance and stay on track spiritually is to pass on what you know to others. The Bible says, 'Those who help others are helped.' As you pass along your insights, you will get more insights from God. Paul challenges Timothy, 'Now I want you to tell these same things to followers who can be trusted to tell others' (2 Timothy 2:2 CEV). If you know people who haven't discovered their God-given purpose in life yet, it's your job to share with them what has been shared with you. For example, don't just read this devotional and keep it to yourself, share it with your friends. The more you know, the more God expects you to use that knowledge to help others. That's how things are supposed to work in His kingdom. James writes, 'Anyone who knows the right thing to do, but does not do it, is sinning' (James 4:17 NCV). In other words, increased knowledge brings increased responsibility. Passing along the purpose of life to others is more than just an obligation; it's one of our greatest privileges. Imagine how different the world would be if everyone knew their calling. That's why Paul writes, 'If you teach these things to other followers, you will be a good servant of Christ Jesus' (1 Timothy 4:6 CEV). Not only does God want us to live out His purposes, He wants us to help others do the same. That is what assignment-centred living is all about. Regardless of your age, the rest of your life can be the best of your life if you will do this one thing – start living on purpose!

Bible in a Year: *Ezekiel 14-15, Hebrews 10*

Appendices

Appendix A — Using the One-Page Plan to Control Progress for Your Eight Words

The purpose of establishing how you measure performance is so you can produce the 'One Page Plan'.

Produce a version of the plan each year to provide a summary of aims. It sets out where you are now and where you want to be in one year's time. Each plan will vary, depending on what you want to achieve. A sample plan is shown next:

January 2023				
XYZ Practice				
The latest update to our OnePage ™ business plan for the year ended March 2009				
Key Results Profit Turnover New Patients	**Actual**	**Target**	**Comments**	

Key Sales Drivers	**Target/ Actual**	**Key actions**	**Key Cost & cash drivers**	**Key actions**
No. referrals from patients	TBA /	Run list from Exact each month	Profit	
No. new patients	30 /	Target xxx per year	Turnover	
		No. / where from / value to be measured each month		
No. patients lost	0 /	Run report re: deregistered patients each month	Debtors	
	0 /	No. who left for a reason and were regretted – each to get letter from x	Costs above budget – no. of instances	
% treatment plans converted	**100% /**	Calculate % figure of those who said yes vs. total estimates	Value of bleaching	
% converted treatment plans started within 1 month ("excellent service")	**100%/**	% of those who said yes and began treatment within the month	Level of overheads	

% patients who also saw a hygienist in the last month	**100%/**	full list of patients vs. those seeing a Hygienist		
No. complaints	**0 /**			

Key underlying success drivers	Target / Actual	Key actions
Enhancing people's smiles	TBA /	
Patient happiness	TBA/	
Welcome systems	0 /	
In the chair, service touches in place	TBA/	
Post-treatment WOWs	n/a /	All patients after treatment of £1k value and above.
Team study zone	X hours p. m./	One person per fortnight to read the article and present at a team meeting
No. new patient services	2/	
Ideas	x/	One idea per person per month. Ideas to be discussed at team meetings. Quarterly prize for the team member with the most ideas implemented
External team training	x/	Team to complete training matrix
Internal team training	x days p.a./	
Team happiness	5/	Weekly record of mood board taken on Weds. Average mood rating target = 5
Systems	x/	

Our Vision
Our Purpose

The plan starts with your purpose and vision, working up to the expected key results. To achieve these results, various drivers are listed with the actions needed.

Target values are shown for each driver and result, with space to record the actual outcome.

All drivers have systems and team names put behind them. This determines how the figures are obtained and assigns ownership and responsibility.

Appendix B — Solitary Retreat in Scotland, 23rd October 2023

As I sit next to the rippling waters of the loch
And the wondrous, magnificent mountains made of rock
Between the glens, sun shining in my face
This ever-changing, beautiful place
The glistening water and the mossy grass
Let your mind be free at last
Pine trees standing to attention in the greens and the gold
Fulfilling their duty as in times of old
The sun burning off the munros
High and snowy and not allowing sorrow
Two solitary trees guarding the gateway between two expanses of water
Doing their duty in protecting this heavenly altar
The golden trees silent and still
Listening and talking and doing God's will.

How was this created?

It's not for us to question. Just revel in its serene and peaceful deity.

"Rob's eloquent weaving of personal experiences and practical wisdom creates a captivating roadmap, guiding individuals to harmonise their inner quest with a meaningful purpose. A must read for anyone, regardless of their stage in the journey of self-discovery and purpose."

Deepa Vakil, Clinical Director at YOR Dental

www.ingramcontent.com/pod-product-compliance
Ingram Content Group UK Ltd.
Pitfield, Milton Keynes, MK11 3LW, UK
UKHW051245180125
453764UK00017B/152